# ARE YOU WEARING
# MY OTHER SHOE?

# ARE YOU WEARING MY OTHER SHOE?

*Marcia Genoveva Bundalian*

1603 Capitol Ave., Suite 310 Cheyenne, Wyoming USA 82001
1-888-980-6523 | admin@urlinkpublishing.com

URLink Print and Media is committed to excellence in the publishing industry.

Book design copyright © 2022 by URLink Print and Media. All rights reserved.

Published in the United States of America

Library of Congress Control Number: 2022901668
ISBN 978-1-68486-090-6 (Paperback)
ISBN 978-1-68486-091-3 (Hardback)
ISBN 978-1-68486-092-0 (Digital)

24.01.22

# ACKNOWLEDGEMENT

<u>DEDICATED WITH GRATITUDE TO GOD ALMIGHTY!</u>

To my father whose Gift of Pen I alone inherited.
To honor him and make him proud.
To remember him with the deepest love
a daughter can give her father.
To thank him for his unconditional love that have molded me
to who I am today.

To my son Tyrone Matta and daughter Mia
Yoingco whose individuality
guided them to who they have become.
Like my dad, I set them free, to fly, to soar and to explore.
To follow their dreams no matter how far it may seem.

To Marvin Schurgin my confidant for so
many years whose understanding
of my dream is beyond Thank You and whose
belief in my capabilities are expressed
in his admirable support and excitement over my dream come true.

To Moses Nnamani Jnr, my quiet mentor,
my greatest friend for many reasons.
My conscience in my moments of doubts.
My wisdom when I am tested.
Thank you for your eagle eye while you
edited the final stage of my book
and for your humble heart and pureness of your intentions.

**TO GOD BE THE GLORY!**

Me and the camera!

My wonderful parents! Mario Magdaleno Yusi Bundalian, July 22nd. Marciana Valdez Rivera, November 2nd. I was told that my father was already engaged when he saw my mother hit a Home Run at her high school event. He did all he could to meet her and after that he broke his engagement and started courting my mother who lived in Floridablanca, Pampanga which was quite a ways from my dads hometown San Fernando Pampanga. Their courtship and long marriage is remembered with the fondest memories!

My greatest loves and jewels. My priceless gifts from God!
**"MY TYRONE AND MY MIA"**

I have four other sisters but I was the only one who had a Debut. Sometimes one never knows the plans and reasons our parents do for their children. Maybe because I was special in the sense that I am my mother's junior. My father have told me that my mother loved me by naming me after her. My mother's beautiful name was Marciana which is a reflection of her Spanish heritage. My father said to me: Your mother loved you so much she decided to take out the "na" from her name to make yours " Marcia". It never dawn on me how precious my name is, because I grew up thinking my mother did not love me. Now I know.

# I AM WOMAN

By: Marcia Genoveva Bundalian
2001

I am a Woman of many facets,
So easy to remember, so hard to forget.
Like a Diamond that is preciously priceless,
I am always worthy, never worthless.

I am a Rose, beautiful and sweet,
A Pillar of Strength to those who are weak.
I am a Bee buzzing all day long,
I never stop till most of my work is done.

I am a Woman with emotions and fears,
And seldom acts on some things unclear.
I cry when I am sad, and laugh when I am glad,
I even go crazy when my hair is so bad!

I have dreams beyond my reach,
Yet the Power within me sees no defeat.
I strive to get what I want,
And grasp opportunities at any given chance.

I am a Woman of Distinct Personality,
That Command Respect for my Individuality.
I stand proud for what I believe,
And love to give more than receive.

I am a Professional Woman,
With a Passion to Succeed.
I'll even go the extra mile,
To capture and fill any one's need.

There isn't anything I cannot do,
Or any dream I will not pursue.
Open the door for me and I'll be there,
Because I am a Woman who will Dare!

# ARE YOU WEARING MY OTHER SHOE?

**"Life is not about the Challenges we encounter.**
**It's the Wisdom to go around them, underneath them,**
**alongside of them or facing then head on to."**
**~Marcia Genoveva Bundalian~**

If I had the magical power to pick the ideal man who will totally and literally take my heart off my chest, I would end up choosing no one! Women are not easy to please and men are more often than not, are never pleasers. They have no clue!

But what makes it worse is that we do not tell them what we really want because we expect them to know. Wrong! Men do not know nor care to know. If it is not interesting to them they do not want to know, more so waste their time talking about it.

You can sulk all day and not speak a word, while your insides are all twisted and the veins on your neck are ready to pop out. They don't care – they go about doing their own thing as they whistle a happy tune drink beer and watch TV. We, on the other hand are boiling inside every minute and pretty soon the time bomb starts ticking and we explode! The worst part is that they are in wonderment as to what is going on with us. But they would not ask …and before a word is said, off they go to let us cool off.

I have learned after three marriages that the smartest thing to do is know when to strike. Know when the timing is right to have a conversation with your man. Do not talk to them when they are watching their favorite sports, drinking beer with their friends, messing around the garage and most important never during mealtime.

My first husband who I married at age 23 was an immature man who lacked the quality called "responsible". Let us call him Ted. We were young and had no plans to marry that early but circumstances pushed us to it. You see every now and then with the cooperation of my driver and maid the four of us would plan a night of escapade. We would wait until everyone had gone to bed, and then the four of us would sneak into the garage and with all our strength pushed the car quietly and slowly to the street. Once it is out of sight we get into the car and the driver would take control and cruise around the neighborhood or enjoy the moonlight at the Luneta Park, which was close to the well known Manila Hotel. Even at that time of the night, the park was still teeming with people enjoying the evening air while boiled duck egg vendors were trying to make money before they called it a day. Unknown to us, that night was going to be our last escapade and it became a disaster that stemmed from my cousin Lourdes seeing the car being pushed out in the dark and woke up my brother and told him that my father's car was stolen!

This particular time we wanted to celebrate Ted's starting a new job at the outskirt of Manila which would require him to be away for three times a week. So we went for a drive. When we returned, the car barely making a sound, as we approached my parent's house, my heart jumped off my chest!!! All the lights around the house were lit and there in the library, sitting by his huge table and playing solitaire was my father. He too was awakened. Fear engulfed my entire being and I made our driver speed up. I did not know what to do? It was now about 1:30 in the morning and we knew we were in trouble. We circled around the block several times to see if perhaps my dad would have given up and went back to bed. That did not happen and I was now in total fear for any repercussion I was about to face.

Our maid was braver than us. She got off the car and walked back to the house where she was of course interrogated and reprimanded. But she had nothing to lose. I had so much to fear. What can I say to my dad that would make sense? How could I be so stupid to have done such a foolish thing and for what? The more I questioned myself the more I punished myself. I guess it felt better that way because I was already punishing me before the actual one I would get from my dad. Why did I not just walk in the house and faced the consequences? This would be a regret I would carry for the rest of my life. Disappointing my dad and no room for lies was right in front of my eyes. I would never do anything maliciously to hurt my father. He was my shield, my parent who showed how much he loved me especially when my mother and I would disagree. But at age 23, I was not as smart as I should have been so we decided to wait it out till morning hoping for fury to calm down. Wrong!

Left with no choice and mentally tired from thinking of a solution and emotionally upset for what I had put myself into, the driver parked the car in front of Stella Maris College where my younger sister Fatima went to school. The driver took the public transportation as he needed to be back at home to drive my dad to work where he was the Senate Advisor on Public Works, a position he held with such prestige and high esteem that even a turmoil caused by me was not enough reason for him to miss work.

After spending restless and uncomfortable hours in the car sitting and watching for the time her class would start, it finally came. I crossed the street and went straight to the school office and asked if I could see Fatima. I must have looked horrible for I saw in her face the concern she had for me. Without questions and without guilt trips innuendos, she told me they have been waiting for me to come home. I was too scared to even cry and at that moment, all I wanted to do was to go home and feel safe again. She was excused from her class, called my mother from a phone booth and her words consoled me "Mommy said go back now".

Ted drove the car and as we approached our house, we stopped at the very corner so my sister could walk home, see that everything was clear, signaled me with a wave. Soon as she did that I got out of the car, hurriedly walked towards home, my heart in my throat, my emotions were at their height. Walking through that long driveway, I saw the side door of our house open. I pushed it in slowly and when I did that, the door opened wide and my mother stood there and in her hand was a small suitcase. The only words that came out from her mouth as she handed me my little belongings was "Go now. Your brother has a gun and he will kill you!"

I did not know whether I was walking fast or running nor could I see where I was going because my eyes were filled with tears and my heart sunk in total disbelief and sadness. I got into the car and told Ted to drive away quickly without even knowing where we would be going. Now, the moment of fun had turned into a nightmare and my life shuttered into pieces that no matter how much I can gather up, it would never be the same. I was not ready to leave home. Neither one of us were.

I turned to a dear friend of mine, Linda and asked if we could spend some time at her house and she opened her house and arms warmly to me. Having another person to open my heart out and get some advice was a temporary relief, not a solution, but it made me fall asleep although peace inside me was missing. I wanted to be home so badly but the doors have been shut before me. I called my mother a few times asking her to let me come home and all she said was "wait till your father comes back from work".

Ted and I went together to face the consequences we put ourselves into. We were ready for any punishment that my father would bestow upon us and we both decided that marriage was out of the questions. We were not about to take that giant step especially as a result of a foolish action we dared to do.

My father was sitting in the library playing solitaire when we arrived. He raised his head up and I saw in his eyes a look I have never seen before. I walked slowly towards him, bent down to kiss his cheek and he turned away. That was the first and only time my father ever did that to me. I was the apple of his eye, the only child he spent more time with because he had to stay home most of the time for fear of being picked up by the Japanese.

World War II was the most titanic conflict in history. Six long and bloody years of total wars. It involved every major force in a war for global domination and at the end, more than 60 million people lost their lives and most of Europe and large part of Asia lay in ruins. War came suddenly to the Philippines on December 8, 1941 when Japan attacked without warning. The Japanese occupied Manila in January 2, 1942 and its people suffered greatly from Japanese brutality. One of many stories I have heard as a child was during that war Japanese soldiers would visit many homes and would take all the infants, throw them up in the air and using their bayonets, would kill the babies as they came down. That was a fear that my mother carried with her and so like my father, I too was kept hidden inside the house.

### "It is through tough times that God develops our character and who we are in Him."

I was the fifth child of Mario Magdaleno Yusi Bundalian and Marciana Valdez Rivera. My paternal grandparents had Chinese & Armenian ancestry while my maternal side had Spanish ancestry, a beautiful combination which was not prominent in my facial features. I looked more like a Japanese girl which became in later years a sibling teaser. I have often heard they say that my mother brought the wrong baby home or that my mother had an affair with a Japanese Leader or the unthinkable, that she was raped and I was the product of that!

So there we were, sitting across my father's table that looked so gigantic that I could not even reach out to him. It did not register in my memory what conversation or questions we had that time for all I could think of was my aching heart for having disappointed him so much that he even refused my kiss of respect. Then he called me with my pet name and said "Look at me Candy. You both have brought shame and anguish to this house and the only way we can solve this issue is for you to get married". And almost simultaneously we replied "But we do not want to get married. We do not have to get married". And what he said next felt like a knife in my heart "Your mother is very upset over this and this is the solution she wants". There was no room for reasoning, or bargaining anymore. My mother won. She finally succeeded in washing her hands off me, something I could never understand as she treated me differently from the rest of my siblings. Even comments from my aunts that she disliked me because my father spent lots of playing time with me and as I grew older, I became the Apple of my Father's Eyes! Mother did not have to love me, I got enough of that from my Dad.

He told Ted to go home and tell his parents of the decisions made. That afternoon, though I was finally home, it felt like my room was a strange place, a place I have never been before and slowly I realized that my entire life has changed and I had no say to it. I no longer had the chance to find the man my heart would marry. Ted and I married in December 1966.

The one and only consolation I got from this unwanted marriage was having two beautiful and precious children, my son Tyrone and daughter Mia. Everything else in the whole matrimony was void of happiness and contentment. Ted did not know neither was he capable of being a responsible husband and father to our children because he was never ready for that role. He did not have to worry since we almost always stayed with my parents in between his losing and finding a job. "Uncertainty" was his middle name. "Temper" was his Gemini name!

One day I sat down and talked with him about our future and said "One of us must go to the States to improve our lives. Either you go or I go". So he said he would. Through the connection and financial help of my father, he was able to go with a tour group. Once he reached California he would apply for a student's visa, work when not in school and after a year, we will follow. It sounded like a perfect plan and a workable plan. For once, in my eyes our future seemed brighter! We were heading for something more solid and months went by so fast that I could not wait to be interviewed by the American Embassy.

So the day came and with my two toddlers with me we stepped into our future. The interviewer was a very nice man and between his questioning and affirming he dropped a bomb at my face! He said "I am sorry but your husband declared in this paper that he is single" and I gasped in shock! "How could that be sir? Here is our marriage certificate" I said. He took the certificate and looked at me intently and said "The mere fact that your husband lied to us, I am afraid we will not be able to give you a visa because if we did then he would no longer have a reason to return to the Philippines." So with a broken dream and a hurting heart we went home.

I immediately went to my father and told him what happened at the Interview. He consoled me with his kindness and understanding for the anger, disappointment and embarrassment I felt at the embassy. I made an overseas call to California and during our conversation he justified why he put he was single. "That was the only way I could get a visa" was his reply. "Wait another year and try one more time" was his advice. So I took it in. What else can I do? I found a job, took care of my kids and with the help of my parents who would not allow us to leave away from the house. We all felt very safe in their presence and I personally enjoyed living there again.

How could I not? As a child of five years of age, I saw my father work with his team as they built a home for us his family of six children and a wife which he adored from head to toe. It was a huge two-story house with one extra tower where he built the bathroom for my mother because he said she was his Queen and that was her

Throne! There were four very large bedrooms upstairs, but only two bathrooms, one for my Dad and the other for my Mom and as for us their children we had a choice on which one we preferred to use! Downstairs was another bathroom that connects another large bedroom and the library. There in the library was that door that was open when I arrived home that nightmarish morning which suddenly opened and engulfed my entire future as my mother handed me my small suitcase and told me to leave before my brother will kill me! What a sad thought. What a sad part of my young life. How could my mother let my brother control my life? How? She is gone now. She left us on August 17, 1997 and with that she took many sad memories of how I questioned her love for me. I was her hand-me-down child, the little maid that jumped fast when she ordered me to do something. Yet, I was, among her daughters, the only one she ever asked to care for her plants, to give her a neck massage on days when she did not feel well or felt dizzy. I remember her telling me to follow her in their bedroom and asked me to massage her pretty legs that sometimes ached. It seemed to me that she always was picking me to do this and to do that. But never my three other sisters. Just me, the unloved one! But was I really unloved by my mother? Did she not like me at all? Questions in my mind that will never be answered.

The living room was comfortable with a mirrored wall and a beautiful bar that separated both rooms. Next to the dining room was my mother's kitchen, constructed to her liking and annex to that was a dirty kitchen where the cook killed and cleaned live chicken, live catfish, milkfish and mudfish that were always grilled above ambered charcoals. This too had brought back memories of my youth where I would beg the cook to give me something to do. Peel vegetables or cut them up or even take the chicken feathers out of its skin after it had been dipped into boiling water. Chores that involved the kitchen, the garden and sometimes the laundry were enjoyable ones for me. Looking back now I think that my mother picked me among my siblings because she knew I found enjoyment in doing those chores. I would like to believe that she was watching me when I was lost in my own world! Somehow it consoled me.

Before the year was over I made another appointment with the Embassy and again excitement filled our hearts as I called Ted to let him know of the date. About a week before our set date, I received a telegram from him. There before my eyes was a sentence that would shutter my hopes and future of my children. It said "Stop all travel plans. Letter follows" Ted

Without thinking, I placed a collect call to him. A woman's voice answered and she said "Wrong Number!" so I called the operator again and this time Ted picked up the phone. "What do you mean "stop all travel plans?" and he replied without hesitation "the more I think of you coming over the more I think it would not work. We just cannot live together anymore." Then a click.

As I sat in front of my father, telegram on my hand and tears rolling down my face, he asked me, "Why are you crying?" I heard it but I could not believe he was asking me that. Shouldn't this be a reason to cry.? My husband just turned his back on us, how can I not cry? Then it dawned on me. My father was trying to open my eyes and mind that had been blurred by a marriage that had started wrong from the beginning. "You are all staying with us. You keep working and support your children. Your mother and I will be here for you. Do not waste your tears anymore because you have your children and he has nothing!" My father was right. He had nothing. But I was not crying because I was feeling sorry for myself. I was crying because he abandoned his son who was only three years old and his daughter who was only two. I hated him for leaving and turning his back on our kids. I loathed his treachery and his whole being. I painted my heart Black and mourned his absence from our lives.

That night, downstairs where we slept, I waited for everyone to fall asleep. I looked at my children's innocent faces, oblivious to the event that just altered their lives, I watched them with sadness and with determination that I will be both their mother and father.

With the telegram in my hand and a cut up picture of Ted from our wedding album I placed it on a plate, lit a candle next to it, turned off the light and quietly I spoke: "If there is truly a Devil, here is my husband Ted who I am giving to you". With that I took his picture, and without hesitation I placed it on top of the flame, watched it slowly burn as I muttered "You will never be happy, you will never have a steady job and you will never have the love of these two innocent children whose lives you exchanged for freedom. This is my curse on you. Go to Hell! May you never have any children and may your life be miserable!"

I flushed the ashes in the toilet, gave my sleeping little ones a kiss and I crawled into bed. There I lay in thoughts. There were no more tears to shed – just had to face the change of the tide. Peaceful sleep came soon and my heart felt calm!

Next morning, I gathered all our wedding pictures, loose and tucked in an album. One by one I went through each photo and separated those that he was in. Plopped on my bed I slowly picked them one at a time and my scissors went to work. Every photo that we were together in were cut in half, and every photo that he was with family, I covered his face with a masking tape! He no longer belonged in our family and therefore all that is a reminder of his abandonment were totally gone, at least in the confines of my little family. He now belonged in the past and in the present he never will be. I colored my heart with a bright red! The year was 1970!

As a young single parent, I crossed the bridge between good days and rough ones but because we lived with my parents, the burden was lighter and the upbringing of my children were balanced by my father's doting nature and my mother's strictness to my son who also became the Apple of his grandfather's eyes. My daughter Mia was on neutral ground. I was a disciplinarian but they felt my love and knew I will never abandon them. With me they were secure, to them I was mama and papa.

I worked and provided as much as I could for my children, and every now and then would ask for my parent's help. I learned to budget, to sew pajamas for them. The rest had to be bought or sometimes were hand-me-downs from my older sister's children. But that did not bother me for in my heart I knew that when you wear hand-me-downs, you become a humble person, and an accepting individual. While my salary was not much, for me it was enough to feel pride in raising my children by myself and not allowing a bad example to dominate their innocence. I was certain that my kids had my genes and not their father's so I was convinced we were going to be alright, that they would be better off especially without a father who they cannot look up to.

Our lives in due time normalized with the steady, loving ways of my parents. My kids had all they needed but no one but them could tell what was really inside their tiny hearts. They were too young to express the loneliness they felt or the void he had left in their lives. Not once did they asked me about him. They did not need to. They had me and I made sure I filled the void even if it existed in a minute scale. I did not see anything in them that would have caused me to be concerned. I think they were just as happy that the fights were gone.

It was 1972 when the final divorce came from California. Resignation was evident but the pain and the insults inflicted upon me was still there, maybe even with my children. But like those long ago times, they seemed to say in their silence "we know you are hurting Mama." But I must admit that it was a glorious day for me. Finally, the thorn on my sides had been pulled out and I no longer felt the pangs of pains I endured from the time we were forced to marry. He had now become somebody else's challenge and headache and the taste of Freedom from him was sweet. I also knew that someday he will pay for the wrong choice he made, not for leaving me, but for making a broken home for two innocent children because he did not have the character to face his responsibilities. So do other young men and women who were also trapped into un-ripened marriages.

It is very common in some countries for one parent to leave the family in seeking greener pastures abroad. This migration has worked for so many families and have become a beginning of a new and better life. So for us who were left behind, it was a normal expectation that the departing parent would send child support every month. In the beginning it materialized but in small amount only and as months went on, slowly the money came late or in many occasions were less than the usual arrangement to the point of finally stopping altogether.

This became an issue and one day I received a letter from Ted with a "brilliant idea" so he said. Why don't I send the kids over to California and he would take care of their needs? After thinking it over and picturing my life without my children, I hurt inside. I sought the advice of my parents and after sharing their wisdom with me, I was left to make the decision.

So I developed a plan.

I penned a letter to him telling him that I was considering his suggestions but before anything else I had some conditions that he would need to agree with or questions I needed answers to.

1. Are you with somebody now? If so, I want to know who she is and her family background.
2. I want to see my kids every year. Either you send them over to me or you send me a ticket to see them.

The same letter I sent him made its way to the hands of his two sisters who I was close with. Then I waited anxiously for Mr. Postman to bring me his letter. It was a long two weeks. I came home from work and there it was - just waiting for me on top of our dining table. The envelope that would be the messenger of good tidings or more reasons to curse. My hands trembled as I started to open the enveloped. But something caught my eyes. At the Sender corner was a woman's name. Jennifer and with my ex-husband's last name. For

12

a moment I thought "who could this be?" and the letter answered it for me.

She was the one living with Ted and I wondered as to the authenticity of her last name. Could he married her right after we divorce or was she just one of those women who after having sex with their man assume they have earned the right to his last name. It did not matter. So I read on.

She introduced herself and answered my inquiries about her and her family background. The next sentence was the clincher. I had to read it over and over again. She said "As far as sending you a ticket to see your children, I am putting my foot down!"

It felt like all the blood in my body went shooting up and I became so angry my first impulse was to call Ted but then I thought "Why waste my time?" so the next moment a decision was made. He will never see his children again! Never.

I collected myself mentally but not emotionally. I knew that the anger I had felt would linger on for days, for weeks, months, years and even through eternity. The hurt he had inflicted in 1970 came back and the hatred surfaced again.

With shooting pain and insulting hurt, I penned my reply to him. Saying "Who wears the pants in your place Ted? Why did you allow her to reply to me when these are our children and she has nothing to do with them even though she shares your bed? How dare her say she is putting her foot down on my request to see my children, on my terms! How dare you allow her to interfere, you spineless minute living creature!"

For every paragraph she wrote, I had a reply. No stones were left unturned for now my life with my children left no room for forgiveness. He nailed himself on the cross, let her wipe his sweats. Sarcastically, I thanked them both for opening my eyes to an unforgiveable mistake I would have made and the kind of people who would have taken my place in the young hearts of my children.

I dropped the bomb. "We do not need you nor your money. We will get to the United States on our own and you will never see your children again, not ever, if I can help it and so help me God! As I wrote and wrote, no tears even blurred my vision, no tear drop, no sadness, just plain anger and deep gratitude to God for guiding me in the direction I went. He made me see the light at the end of the tunnel. My load was lifted and my focus switch slowly to where I would start a new life, for just the three of us, my two precious gifts that can never be exchanged for the treasures of the world. He lost his battle and I won the war.! His sisters were advised of my decision.

One morning while the children were at play, I took the shoe box where I had stored all the cut up photos of him. Underneath the mango tree, I set the box down and with dried up twigs and a piece of paper, I struck a match and soon the fire of life sparkled before me. One by one I took the pictures from the box and placed them on top of the flame. One by one I saw his life with us turn into ashes. One by one, the pain I had kept for so long burned too.

His name hardly came up. My children, most especially my son Ty were never void of a father figure image because of my father and brother Joey. To this day, my son had carried on his uncle's racing dream and his grandfather's character made him a well respected coach in the kart racing realm. I chose to color my heart White for the purity of love that my children and I shared!

Years went by and we were happy. We still lived with my parents who doted on us and I stopped expecting child support from Ted who I found out later on was having problems keeping a job. Wasn't that what I wished on him? Deep inside I was pleased. I learned also that the very same woman who replied to my letter was thrown out by Ted's father after he found out what she had done. "Did the devil really hear my plea that night?" I wondered but did not care. I always believed that when someone does you wrong, like a wheel, it will come back to run that person down, and slowly that theory seemed to have proven itself.

It did not take long before his name ever came up during our family conversations and neither one of my children bothered to ask. Just as quickly he dropped us out of his life, so did we. Once in a while I would go out to socialize through quiet dinners or dancing but never did it come to my mind about having another man in my life. It was not because I still hoped for Ted but because I was still angry at him for his betrayal, abandonment and selfish act of immature freedom!

It was in the summer of 1974 when a friend of mine, Bert asked me to join him and his wife Maryanne for dinner. He was entertaining his father's business partner and he thought it would be a great idea to meet him. He was a New Yorker. So after talking to my parents and my kids, Bert came to pick me up and we proceeded to the Hilton Hotel. I asked him where Maryanne was and he said she would just meet us there as she wanted to tuck their children to bed. I thought what a loving mother!

While waiting at the lobby I briefly found out who this man was who I was about to meet. He was Jewish, an only child and he owned a Placement Agency in New York. He comes to Manila every four months to interview nurses, process their papers and place them in many different States except California. How he looked like I never asked. After all this was just an innocent one time dinner!

From where we sat I could see the elevators and soon enough, a tall white man wearing white pants and long sleeves shirt walked out of the elevator and with such a beautiful smile, he approached us, shook Bert's hand and then turned to me. Bert went through the formality of it all. Marcia. This is Lee Kramer and I stood there feeling nothing but wonderment as to where Maryanne was.

I could not help notice that the top button of his shirt was not buttoned and there in his lightly hairy chest rested a Chai. That drew my curiosity but I did not venture to ask anything about it. We headed for the dining room, my head still turning around to catch glimpse of Maryanne. No luck. We sat at a cozy booth, me in the middle and in between drinks I would ask Bert about Maryanne and he would say, "She should be here soon. Why don't we order now and she can order when she comes?". So we did.

Dinner came and went and no Maryanne but it did not matter to me anymore as the conversation around the table was great, Lee was a charmer and a talker and most of all was full of jokes. We were roaring with laughter and the ice was broken. I felt at ease with him and I knew that with or without Maryanne, Bert will soon take me home. Then Bert decided to call Maryanne so he excused himself as we continued exchanging funny stories. When he came back he said he just spoke with her and she did not feel like driving alone at night so Bert opted to pick her up and said he would return right away. Dessert was accompanied with more laughter and Lee's interest was to know more about me. Without spilling my whole life story to him, I gave him enough reason to feel that his blind date was worth the eyes of the beholder. His demeanor was of a gentleman and his blue eyes were speaking something that was happening in his heart. I pretended not to notice, after all, this was just a dinner date.

He suggested that we should move to the lounge area where dancing was as inviting as swimming in a heated pool with a glass of wine to cool you down. Oh, yes, from dinner to dancing, I sipped my wine as I cranked my neck looking for Bert and Maryanne. As soon as Lee noticed my concern he would ask me to dance again and we boogied, rock and rolled and cha-cha-chad to the delightful music of the band.

President Ferdinand Marcos declared Martial Law in 1972 and in 1974 it was still running very strong. Nobody was allowed to be on any streets after midnight. Anyone who was caught was taken to jail and released the next day or so after being reprimanded and disciplined. It did not matter who you were – his law bear no exception. Only the military roamed the dark nights of the streets, like prowlers waiting for their preys.

I looked at my watch and it was eleven thirty and with a good taxi driver, I could make it home before midnight. I realized then that Bert and Maryanne were not going to show up. Maybe they had a fight I thought. Maybe she got lazy and just decided to stay home. No matter what the reasons were, it was not important at all because I had to get going because Bert left me stranded.

Anxious, upset and fuming mad at Bert, I told Lee I was going to take the cab and head home. He would not hear of it. He was not going to let me take a chance and end up in jail So he suggested we go up his room. I said I would just sit in the lobby and leave as soon as the curfew was off. He was not happy with the idea and convinced me that he would be in his best behavior and would feel better knowing I was safely tucked in his bed while he slept on the couch.

Not having much of a choice I caved in not only because I knew he was a gentleman and trusted him but also because of my own fear of what could happen to me in the hands of those military men who have abused women they had caught after midnight. Worst scenario was if he could not resist the temptation at least I knew I am so desirable. But I did feel safe around him and left it that way.

So he extended his hand to me, I reached out for it and we walked towards the elevators. Door opens, we walked in. I saw him press #22 and soon we were moving. About halfway on, I felt my legs turning cold, my vision became blurry and the elevator walls begun to spin. I grabbed his arm and leaned hard on him as I said "I am going to faint ".

He put his arm around me, held me very close as I hanged on to dear life. The elevator door opened and Thank God, his room was just a few steps from the elevator and supporting me so I would not drop to the floor became a struggle for him to put in the key. Finally, it opened and the only thing I remembered was me falling to my face at the foot of the bed!

When I woke up, I was fully clothed and lying down on one side of the bed. On the night table was the ice bucket and two face towels. Lee was tenderly applying the wet and cold towel on my forehead. I would go in and out of my sleep until I finally lost it and was completely out!

It was about 8:00 in the morning when I was awakened by movements in the room. Lee was up and was all dressed to go to the agency for the first phase of the interview. Once again, Lee showed me his tender side and total concern for my well being. He said the car was on its way to pick him up and that I should just rest and when ready call for room service. He kissed me on the cheek, held my hand and sweetly said "call the office when you are ready to go home so I can send the car over ". He did not want to leave me but he had work to do. I could tell from his never ending "see you later" And "I will put the "do not disturb sign" so you can go back to sleep".

As soon as the room service delivered my lunch and left, I called the agency and asked for Lee. I was told he was busy interviewing and the next voice I heard was Bert teasingly asking "What happened to you last night? You scared him bad". Boy, did I give Bert a good piece of my mind. It was then I realized it must have been set up that way from the start with Maryanne not really joining us and Bert and Lee playing along with their scheme. But what they did not expect was the way it ended without any planning! While it was an embarrassing moment for me, it gave me a chance to see who Lee really was and the kind of gentleness he possessed. I think he fell in love with me that night! Bert sent the driver to pick me up and soon I was home telling my mother what happened to me and then I was asleep again.

By 3:00 pm Lee was already calling me to see how I was feeling and to ask if I would have dinner with him again. My eyes were still heavy and my body needed more rest so half awake I told him I would. He arrived at 6:00 in the evening and with the eagerness of smiles anyone could ever seen. He met my parents for the first time and he was so impressed with them especially with the kind of home we had, simple yet wealthy with warmth. He also saw in that brief moment how we lived, not in luxury but in comfort and with all the household helps my parents needed to make their life easy. I believe that it was then that Lee knew he was not going to lose a chance with me. Courtship was not limited to me alone, it extended to my parents, brother, sisters, cousins, relatives and my son Tyrone and daughter Mia. The chemistry was instant and mutual. For the rest of his stay we saw each other everyday and dinner every night.

When he finally left for New York after two weeks, I basically expected him to disappear from my life. I did not entertain a bit of hope for I was not looking for a serious relationship while I was still angry inside and did not think that any other deep emotions would be possible. Besides I felt that long distance relationships was not for me. I love being loved everyday! I colored my heart purple.

To my surprise and delight, Lee wrote me every week and each letter or card were filled with dreams of me ~ how I have affected his life, how happy he was and how lucky he was! My heart began to see pink. His sincere confession of love and affection and need for me to be in his life turned my feelings for him around. Now he became someone I could spend the rest of my life with. My blind date became for real and so begun the purest of romance and unfailing courtship connecting us many miles away.

Every four months Lee came physically into my life. Every single night we dined together, sometimes by a candlelight or other times with friends and family. Regardless of the situation, we were one and the enjoyment of each other's touch became second nature to us. He doted on me, adored me from head to toe, showered me with his thoughtfulness in gifts and electrifying embrace. His eyes always spoke of his tender love and even a kiss on my forehead trinkled down very adoring showers of comfort. But his thoughtfulness spread beyond me and found its way in my children, parents and sibling. He adapted to us and he was lovingly adopted by my family.

For all those times Lee went back to New York, my heart felt such emptiness from his warm affection- but reality was also in front of me. After all, he was not a free man at that time so I did not bank on our future together and contented myself to seeing him whenever he returned. I did not build further expectations nor did we talk about it but I knew he had now fallen in love with me. But was that enough for me and my children? Where was our future heading to? How long must I wait?

Prior to my meeting Lee, a friend of mine met with a group of Canadian Investors who were interested in the aircraft industry. She invited me to join them and had a great time. Fred with deep blue eyes and almost perfect nose showed some interest in me. He was full of charm especially when he spoke and laughed. But there was no spark , no attraction, no chemistry. Just plain acquaintance was all he earned so when he invited me to dine with him alone, I accepted. I felt safe knowing there were no emotions involved and he respected my wish that we just remain friends. Wisdom was also knocking on my head saying "his future is uncertain and he has nothing to offer" and I listened!

Months went by and every now and then we would talk. It was here that I found out that after all the meetings they had held, there was nothing solid or futuristic with their investments. Slowly they backed out, one by one until Fred was left all alone. He had no money and he was stuck. There was nothing I could or would do. He was on his own and I felt so sorry for him.

One morning, while working at the Manila Stock Exchange, a beautiful vase of roses arrived and the delivery boy asked for me. With joyful curiosity I opened the card and I gasped as I read:

"I'll see you at dinner tonight "
Love,
Lee.

My heart sung all day long though it seemed like eternity to me. I took a break just so I could call him at the hotel. When he picked up the phone my heart pounded like warrior drums and even before I could say anything, he said "I wanted to surprise you ". I melted.

By seven in the evening, Lee arrived at my parent's house. I did not have to be there to witness his entrance as my parents were looking forward to meeting him and being very gracious people, I could just imagine how they would have been taken by him. Lee was a natural and exuded an aura of self-confidence and sincerity. My mother went to get me and with Tyrone and Mia tugging on to me, I gave Lee a loving and welcoming hug, an appropriate gesture in front of my parents and kids.

As he gazed at me I saw the sparks in his blue eyes that told of his excitement and ease. Before he arrived, I took my kids aside and told them I was going to dinner with a special friend and that they could watch TV for a while but must go to bed when their nanny tells them to do so. They seemed to feel my heart for they promise to do so knowing I would be back and never abandon them like their father did. Before Lee and I left, I tucked them in and kissed them goodnight.

As soon as we drove away, Lee pulled me close to him, wrap his arms around me and the only thing I felt was his passion that ran over my spine. He told me how much he missed me and how he longed to touch my silky skin again, smell my hair, caress me from head to toe. It was heavenly, just him saying it and I felt so secure with his hand tenderly holding mine.

For a brief moment of silence, my thoughts went back to my parents. How did they really feel about him? Have they accepted him as my suitor? What were their expectations? Did they see him as my knight in shining armor? Did they even asked him his marital status? I could not wait for the morning to come so I could sit with them and get some assurance that they have accepted Lee for who he was and what he was bringing into my life. How would they feel if I told them that Lee was a married man? Would they ask me not to see him again or would they respect my choice? No matter what it was going to be, I made up my mind. I would continue to see Lee, enjoy his company and not bank on anything and most importantly, I would never ask him to leave his wife for me!

Dinner was as always, wonderful. Just the warmth of his being surrounding me sent such deep feeling of comfort and ease. I began to see more in the way he gazed at me how much he enjoyed my company and as if time was not enough for him to have me completely. The thought of leaving me behind again reflected in his eyes that spoke of love. We avoided talking about it and just embraced the moment we were together as we danced all night as though the dance floor was only meant for us.

One evening, much to his dislike, he had to go with his partner to dine with business associates so he arranged for me to have room service which I did not mind at all. It was going to be a quiet time with myself, a good time to just relax and perhaps call some friends to catch up on what is new. Lee would be back before I even knew it. After dinner I made some calls and one of them was to my friend Fred who I had not spoken for sometime. So we talked for a while and then he asked me if I would meet him downstairs and just stroll with him along the streets around the hotel. I told him that Lee would be returning soon and I did not want to be out but he pleaded and promised it won't be a long walk. So I met him and we just walk along one way and turned around to walk back. As we talked, I kept looking at the cars passing by for reason I could not understand why but I was to find out soon enough. For there in one of the cars was Lee and his partner sitting at the back of the car, him looking outside at people walking on the sidewalk. For that split seconds our eyes met. I froze. The car kept going and I began to panic. "What would he be thinking? "

All I remember at that moment was saying to Fred "I have to go, I have to go "and I started to run towards the hotel. I never once looked back for I did not care. All that was going through my mind was "how can I make him see that we were just walking and talking"? "What have I done"?

I slowly opened the door, my heart pounding with unidentifiable emotion and it sunk. Lee was not in the room. I called the hotel lounge thinking that would be a good place to find him and asked the bartender to page him. My heart lifted as I heard his voice but my tongue was twisted as I tried to say too many words that sounded sorrowful. I said "What are you doing there? Would you please come up"? He answered in a very controlled voice "Let me just finish my drink ".

I sat at the edge of the bed, nervous as hell yet confident I can make him understand what just happened but in my mind I questioned "would he believe me ... really believe me?" The waiting seemed forever, the silence deafening. My heartbeat and heavy breathing were all that I could hear as I fixedly gazed at the door, waiting in anticipation for the latch key to turn. I would hear footsteps outside the door but they continue walking, then silence again. I called the hotel lounge again and this time in a much relax voice he said "I will be there in a minute ".

I started to have a one-way conversation with myself "what should I do first? Should I just run to him, make passionate love to him and then explained later or should I just bawl like a mad woman and in between sobs explained what really happened or should I just let him know how much I love him.?" But fear was the answer and the thought of an ending to an affair so young was right before me!

I stiffened as I heard the key turn and if someone had barely touched my shoulders at that very moment, an ambulance would have been called. Slowly he opened the door, his face sunken and his blue eyes sad. I jumped up and hugged him and kissed him on the cheeks. He held me tight, a good sign I silently thought. Then he sat me down on the bed and waited for me to say something and I did. Between sobs and "I am sorry" I explained to him what transpired and who Fred was. This was not the time to hold back any details that led to the truth. In my mind I figured if I told him exactly what this was all about and he still feels hurt or betrayed at least I know in my heart I told him the truth and if we were to part, then our relationship was not meant to last at all.

I held his big hands tightly with mine and felt that warm secured feeling I felt each time we held hands. Almost simultaneously we both looked towards the door as the sound of paper being slipped through the door dominated that one single second. Someone had pushed an envelope under the door and there it lay, like a mystery. Lee got up and opened the door. There was no one there. Then he picked up the envelope, handed it to me and there in big hand-written letters was "MARCIA". Nothing else was written anywhere in the envelope. Without knowing what to expect I slowly tore the opening and pulled out one long letter written on a ruled memo pad. There at the bottom of the page was a name I was so familiar with ....Fred. I handed the letter to Lee and asked him to read it to me.

The letter was filled with bitterness and carried a tone of anger and jealousy towards someone who was the recipient of my affection which he never had the chance with me. Funny how in that short moment of bewilderment, Fred was able to gather some information as shown on his letter. Part of it said "Beware of Jewish men bearing gold and silver for they will buy your love with them". He said a lot of hateful things about Lee and I guessed it was done out of simple jealousy and bitterness.

That unexpected letter proved to Lee I was telling the truth and that there was friendship that bonded us, nothing else. That night we went to bed in silence, each lost in our own minds and thinking of what next step to take. In my mind he was still a married man and I could just walk away.

Morning came and the room still was filled with gloom. He said he did not want breakfast but for me to order room service and that he would call me sometime during the day. Back at the Manila Stock

Exchange I buried myself with work, trying to put up a face so the sadness in my heart would not show but my ears were eager to hear the phone ring. Just before lunch Lee called. He asked me to have dinner with him and though I was wanting to do that I held back and told him I would have to think about it. As soon as the market closed I headed home totally perplexed and emotionally divided.

I needed sleep and some time to think things over. It had come to a point where a decision was in view.

**"Let yourself feel the pain and then review the consequences. What are your losses? What would you like to recover?**

My thoughts were interrupted with the ringing of the phone. It was Lee's business partner who happened to be a friend and contemporary of my father. He wanted to talk with me about Lee so he tried to put some sense into my confused mind. He told me how Lee was suffering inside, how troubled he was about last night and how much he loved me. Mr. Lim's words echoed in my ears as he said: "Marcia, think of what each of these men can offer you and your kids. Lee has a successful business and absolutely loves you or he would not feel this rotten inside. What can that Canadian offer you? With Lee you have a chance for a better life in the United States". I wanted to say "how can I go to the United States when Lee is still married?" His voice at the other end snapped me from my thoughts. "Think this out seriously. You have a future with Lee. Have dinner with him tonight so you can talk".

Before I could answer him I heard Lee's voice at the other end. "Would you please have dinner with me tonight? I really need to see you and if you come without your overnight bag then I will know how you feel about me but if you do, you will not be sorry you did. What time shall I send the driver for you? Please Angel, please see me tonight."

Still unsure of what I would do I consulted with my aunt who in her wisdom said to me: "Think of what Marcia wants. How honestly do you feel about Lee? Do you believe he loves you? From what I have seen since you met him, he has been so devoted to you and sees no one else but you. He dotes on you … adores you … loves you!" I listened to my aunt but most of all, to my heart that I have slowly gifted to Lee.

The driver came at seven o'clock and I left to have dinner with the man who has fallen in love with me, my knight in shining armor who would not allow anyone to woe me, more so, be with me. Lee was so attentive and as loving and joyful as we dined. The incident was never brought up and all through the night, as we danced, he held me tight, and as we cuddled next to one another, I felt so secure in his embrace and very loved as he touched my body and soul.

Before we both drifted into sleep, he pulled me over and held me close, kissed my forehead and said "thank you for bringing your overnight bag". We were one once again!

**"Commitment is doing the thing you said you would do,
long after the mood you said it in, has left you!"**

I had gotten so used to Lee coming in and out of my physical life so whenever he left for New York, there only existed warm hugs of gratitude for having been together again and that gnawing and giddy feeling that in three months we would be in each others arms once more. The evening we dined last he told me that as soon as he returned to New York, he would open his own post office box for privacy reasons and to stop using his secretary's home address. So for the rest of the following three months we exchanged letters every single week! Letters of love and missing each other and wanting to be together forever dominated any business or family news. We were very much in love, eager to start a new life where harmony, honesty and happiness rules our home and our relationship. I knew that my overnight bag sealed what his heart felt and what we shared without any tinge of doubt.

Lee was a gift-giving man. He spoiled me rotten as well as my children, Tyrone and Mia and not to forget my parents and every now and then, my siblings too. So on his next visit he surprised me with a huge briefcase that he placed on the bed. My curiosity was killing me. In my mind I was asking why would he bring me a briefcase and as big as that! With his mischievous smile he urged me to open it pointing to me where to start. As I opened the case, I was overwhelmed with what I saw. Inside that briefcase was a stereo set. The two separated covers with the speakers, there was a record player, a cassette player and a cartridge player .... all in one big briefcase. He also took out some cartridges and pop one in the slot and music filled the room. He knew how I loved music and here is my love showing me once more how important I was to him that he made it a point to really know me well. More gifts came out from his luggage, beautiful and expensive clothes from New York and some jewelries too.

That evening we decided to go out for dinner and as we entered the already full elevator, he was smiling. I knew he was up to something. There is always that certain smile and sideway look in his eyes that I recognize and silently prepare for. As the elevator started to go down, he pulled out from his pocket a $5.00 bill and with the silliest smile he could make, he loudly said "Thank You for a lovely evening" as he went through the motion of extending his hand that held the $5.00 bill. The reactions from the crowd told it all, as I pushed his hand gently and said "No thank you, that was on the house". I guess because we were now giggling, the crowd knew it was not for real and they laughed with us. But I was not done with him. As soon as we stepped out of the elevator, him still laughing for putting me in such embarrassing moment, I told him "let's put this in another point of view ... others may have thought "what a stingy man" or "poor girl she got a loser" or simply put "bad ass foreigner". We never stopped talking about it and each time we did we were rib aching from laughing. That would be one of the endearing reason why I loved Lee. They say "marry a man who can make you laugh when you are feeling low or just need a quick "Picker Upper". Yes, he made me laugh and I miss him so and still ask "why did you leave me?"

I had learned to play along with his love for pranks. It really did not affect our relationships as I learned to take life lightly especially now that I have someone loving me with such tenderness. But I vowed revenge one of these days so it came.

It was a rainy evening and we just wanted to cuddle up and be comfy so we ordered room service. Dinner was wonderful and it made me think of getting even with him for all the many embarrassing times he had put me through. I pretended that I saw a cockroach by the trash can as I screamed and climbed the bed. Chivalry was on sight. He jumped from his chair and bent over looking for the insect and I kept pointing to him where to look. As he was bent over I took a piece of meat from our dinner and threw it at him. Bullseye! Hit the target! He jumped so high as a man would scream and that sound kept ringing in my ears for days as I rolled back and forth on the bed with rib aching laughter! He then realized there was no cockroach! What a wonderful end to a rainy evening night!

Lee was for real. He lived a life where emotions dwell and he knew how to identify them. There was never a dull moment with him. He adored me and loved me like no one has done before. In him I felt safe. In him I found a man of my dream. But he was still not free and I had to hold back the love I had for him. Getting hurt again was not in my agenda.

His next visit was more memorable than the others for the simple reason that a new chapter in my life and my kids was about to embark. Before we retired that night he sat me down and for the first time he became very serious, yet his voice sounded like a song to me as he said "I have filed for divorce". I found myself just looking into this man's blue eyes as they slowly became teary as he watched a tear go down my cheek! We embraced for a long time, not saying a word but listening to our hearts that had turned joyful. He said the whole process will be over soon because it was going to be an easy divorce. I asked him how he knew that to be so. He took a bundle of photos from his briefcase and handed them to me. He moved closer to me as together we viewed the photos that would very soon set him free!

The photos were taken of his wife and their salesman when they went to Africa on a business trip and photos taken at local motels where the hired detective put markers that would indicate whether they stayed in all night together as suspected. The photos painted thousands of words. Photos of holding hands, kissing and simply doing things lovers do. Lee had the Aces. She lost as an adulteress. Lee was removed from a relationship that was poisoning him slowly. He was able to spit out the venom that was controlling his existence and while he would have wanted to have won custody over his own son, it was not to be, He was ordered by the court to pay child support!

Before Lee left for New York, he spoke to my parents and told them what was going on and then he asked them for my hand in marriage. They gave their blessings and approval with all the love they now had for him. Lee's life was now taking a new turn and I was there standing, waiting for the love of my life! All the days that followed were filled with plans for us and my kids. We would soon be one happy family once we got to the States. I now had let go of my exiled feeling of love and my world became clear blue as the sky and my heart tickled pink!

**"Lord, don't let me remain where I am. Help me reach where You want me to be!"**

As soon as his divorce was over, Lee petitioned for me and my children. We were approved right away but we had a predicament, a situation I refused to entertain in my mind and he preferred not to talk about. But we had no choice. The issue was right before our eyes and we could not move forward until we sat down and and took the matter headstrong. It was a determining factor that would affect all of us, most specially my children.

When he came back, all sorts of emotions were flying about. There were moments when all that mattered was our future but then again, as quickly as it came, so it went away. There were more important and delicate issues we had to face and so we did.

After a wonderful dinner at my parents house, we dismissed the kids and we sat in the living room with my dad and mom. They were still glowing with happiness as they looked at us with such approval and excitement. My heart was pounding and Lee was as calm as can be. I took a deep breath and said "Mommy, Daddy, there is something we would like to discuss with you regarding my kids". My dad said "I am glad you brought that up because your mother and I have something to say to both of you too. We have been thinking and considering this new life you are about to embark to. You and Lee are just starting a life together and we would like to help you make that path a little easier. We thought it would be best for the children to stay with us first until you have settled down and ready to have them over. We will look after them and care for them and you need not worry about them. We also want them to spend some time with us before you take them away".

My father's voice sounded almost like a plea and as I looked at his face, I saw that sadness I did not want to see. I knew that deep inside his loving heart, there was a tinge of pain knowing he was going to miss my presence as much as he would my children. While his words were soothing and so naturally spoken, I felt my heart sink and my mind wondered how I could be without them in my life. How could I abandon them? Would they really understand? Was I being just like their father, only thinking of my own good? They are still babies ... how could I leave them even in the care of the most wonderful parents in the world? I did not realize I was crying until Lee handed me his handkerchief.

With Lee's hand on mine he spoke words I wanted to hear. They were filled with genuine love for my children and honorable gratitude towards my parents. He too started to cry as he could not believe what my father had said. He was so touched by the sensitiveness of my parents and their deep desire to usher us into a smooth union. It was a moment of truth, of acceptance, of guidance and true unconditional parental love! That night we took Tyrone and Mia with us to the hotel who delighted in the thought of going swimming the next day. Their innocence pinched my heart and I asked again "how can I leave them behind?"

That night, Lee and I were in tight embrace as we removed the sadness of the night from our minds and settled it in our hearts where we knew it will rest for a while until we have them back in our arms again. The morning after was like a brand new day. We did not have a care as we watched our little ones enjoy themselves throughout the day. After dinner, we had another task to face. This time it will not be as easy.

As expected both Tyrone and Mia listened intently to what I had to say to them. Young as they were then, their attention span was amazing and their understanding of what I had said seemed to have sunk in their little hearts. "Mama will have to go with Papa Lee very soon and you will have to stay here with daddy and mommy for a while. It will not be very long and I will come back to get you" I said. "Where are you going Mama" they asked. "To New York. I have to take a plane to get there because it is very far. You will take the same plane when I come back to get you" I answered, as my throat started to tighten up. I held their tiny hands and cupped them closed. I wanted my children to feel my heartbeat as I gently pressed my palms on their so beautiful hands. I wanted them to be assured that I love them more than anything in this world and that I will never turn my back on them even if it meant being just a kept woman for Lee.

There were no tears shed that night but I was fighting my emotions internally. They were still babies and here I am embarking on another journey without them. Was I doing the right thing, I asked myself as I watched their innocence lost perhaps in a dream or their simplicity and strength take over what I had told them. Everyone I love lay there sleeping peacefully as if there were no problems that came about this new step I was about to take. Finally, I closed my eyes and put my life in the palms of God's hands.

**"Dream whatever you desire to dream.**
**Go wherever you wish.**
**Seek whatever your heart dictates..**
**Because Life is Unique and is dependent on**
**how you shape it."**

The month of December 1976 was probably the most nerve-wrecking, emotionally draining time for me. For Christmas I doted on my kids. Spending extra money, instead of penny-pinching, to buy something they really would love to have. I was covering the void of the following Christmas in case we were not ready to have them join us in New York. My children have made it easy for me to tackle this dreadful separation by just being children, oblivious to their mornings and evenings without me sleeping in the same room with them. All I had to do was look at them and my heart would sink again and again, deeper and deeper each time. But when I see them with my parents and the attention they showered them, I forced myself to release the sadness inside of me knowing they would be in very loving home and hands.

Christmas day was all festive with my other siblings coming by, bringing more gifts to all and special lunch which my mother had the cook prepare for us. The cousins were all joyful, frolicking at my mom's beautiful garden all laughing, as they played all day. Inside the house the atmosphere was a bit different. We were talking about my leaving for New York. That night I could not sleep. I wanted to stay up and just sit and watch my babies sleeping. My heart ached knowing the following night I would be in flight, crying myself to sleep as I await my arrival at JFK Airport and down the steps would be my love Lee! Sleep was a waste of time. I tried to savor their baby smell and wished I could put it in a bottle so I could just take a whiff of it before I cried myself to sleep.

It was a long 24- hour straight flight. Lee made sure my departure and mid-air emotional state of mind would be calm knowing I just had to keep sleeping only to wake up in his arms. I knew Lee was going to be a nervous wreck by the time I arrived. He worried too much about me. I guess it was of his deep love and concern for me as he saw how I struggled to accept the temporary separation I would have with my children. But he was determined to change the course of my life … he was determined to spend the rest of his life with me and my precious children..

One thing about me is that no matter what state of mind I am in, food seem to soothe my body and so I ate whatever the flight attendants offered me. I knew that I had to nourish my body and mind so I may be able to weather whatever comes my way. So I slept some and ate some and soon we landed in New York. As we taxied to the gate my thoughts awakened and my heart was beating two different beats: one of sadness and the other, happiness. How can I be happy when I am so sad? But why should I be sad when I should be very happy for there waiting on the steps was the man I love who had filled a part of my empty life with so much love and hope for our future.

His face lit up as I came down the escalator. His smile was a sight to see and there standing next to him was his ten year old son, also beaming with a smile. For a moment my sad face smiled and as I got closer to them my heart sunk again. The very sight of his son brought me immediately back to my children and realizing that, I pulled myself together and gave both of them the warmest hug I could give. But Lee's hug was what changed my whole feeling that moment and all I could think of was hugging him back and I did. I was home.

We got married in the morning of March 9, 1977 in a Judge's chamber. I cannot think of any reason why during the brief ceremony I started to giggle inside and the moment our eyes met I lost it. I burst into laughter, then Lee laughed too and soon the Judge and his wife were giggling too. No one knew the reason why but now that I look back I think it was a way for me to release my nervousness. But it did not matter for what was important was Lee laughed with me and that said a lot that morning.

We walked out the Judge's chamber as man and wife. There was nobody there but us. It was so special because we wanted it that way. It was a very quiet wedding until we arrived at the restaurant where everyone was waiting for us. There was not one silent moment left after that. It was a joyful time even without the presence of my children. I just held them close inside me, just for me, no one else! We did not have the money for our honeymoon and that was fine with me. New York was almost a honeymoon place for me and the thought of saving money for my children's arrival was enough for me.

Before we got married, Lee started his own business called RANK International. It was a very small office and we had a secretary, he made me the Vice-President and we recruited nurses from the Philippines and provided jobs for them all over the States except California. Business was good but we were together too much and it was creating a discomfort between us so he talked me into opening a clothing store in Northern Boulevard. It was going to be a store that the neighborhood could afford to buy from, mainly jeans and T-shirts. This concept changed as we started going to the garment industry in Manhattan where we saw better looking clothes. So we upped the quality of our merchandise and raised the price as well. It was a welcome change for some but not enough to make a big killing.

One Saturday night at about eleven o'clock the store alarm went off so Lee and his son-in-law Lowell drove to the store to check it out. By the time they arrive, the cops were already there casing the area. Nothing. It was presumed that because there was a railroad track behind the building, they thought the alarm could have been triggered by the train coming by. So they close the shop and went home. At about 3:00 that morning, the alarm went off again so Lee and Lowell went to check it out. This time the cops were there again so Lee decided to unplug the alarm and get it checked when office hours opened. Tired and frustrated, he finally went back to sleep. No more alarm to wake him.

Got up quite early Sunday morning to drive to Manhattan. It was the only day I did not have to be at the store and that day was shopping day for new clothes. We bought more designer jeans and tops and a few nice affordable dresses. On the way back Lee asked me if I would like to put the price tags at the store or at home and I opted the latter. One day away from the store was a good chilling out time. But because the price tag tool was at the store, we had to stop there to get it. I stayed in the car and Lee went inside. He came back so fast, his face was without color and his eyes were strikingly upset. He said to me "we might as well close the store" and to make me understand, he waved me out of the car, put his arms around me and walked me to the store. There on the floor were left-over merchandise that the burglers did not take or were not able to take. All the expensive jeans were gone. The store was stripped and they left a mess. We looked around for any clue and did not see anything that showed they went through the door. What I saw next chilled my spine and I called Lee immediately. The ceiling had a big hole where they came in and worked like a team, as they pass to each other every merchandise they could take. They must have been at the rooftop when Lee and Lowell came to check the store. They must have been lying flat on the rooftop so the cops would not see them and I thought that they must have waited for the train to pass as they slowly sewed the ceiling off.

All legal proceedings were made with the cops and the landlord. This was actually the fourth time the alarm went off and we rationalized that the first three false alarms were caused by the train's vibration as it passed through the night and we never thought of turning the alarm off.

We went back to the house, feeling beaten, losing without a fight, succumbing to the malicious deeds of people who had no respect for others. We were angry. We were sad. We were mad as hell. We sat down and seriously calculated our next move. The cops were not hopeful about finding these kids who invaded our privacy. We had nothing but piles of clothes we just bought and some that were left on the floor of the store. Soon we found ourselves rationalizing the situation and started talking sensibly. We were closing shop! That was it. We felt that the store had basically taken away week-ends from us and Lee after working five days a week at the office, still comes to be with me at the store on Saturday and Sunday. That is when I stay home to do all household chores that could not be attended during the week. By the time we had dinner, we were exhausted. So it was time to let go of the store.

We opened Marcee's of Manila on February 1979 and we closed it on December 1979. To gain some financial help, we sold everything in the store at a discounted price. We did not want to have one single merchandise unsold and we did. While we lost the business to the tune of $20,000 for such a very short time we psyched ourselves to let it go because we got each other back and our lives became normal again. We agreed that it is not all about money but the happiness we can offer each other on a day to day basis was all that we needed.

Tragedy struck our family in very sad ways: I lost my younger sister Fatima to breast cancer in 1978 and in 1979 Lee lost his mother who I dearly loved, to a stroke. I did not know then that in 1980 I was going to lose the most precious man in my life.

My sister Fatima was very young when she followed her equally young husband to the United States. They lived in Chicago, Illinois and were a happy family with the arrival of their first born son Manny Boy. It did not take long for their solid family to shutter. He became verbally and physically abusive to my sister and with the help of some drugs changed their relationship. Then their second son Jong-Jong arrived to a very turmoiled family structure. My mother who flew from the Philippines to be with my sister told me stories of discomfort as she witnessed the stressful life of my sister whose so sweet and calm personality changed to parallel her husband's emotional up and down stream ways.

I do not know how my sister did it but she did! I am sure that after a lot of soul searching and reality checks, they decided to let my mother bring Jong-Jong with her back to the Philippines where he would be in the care of her mother-in-law. He was born on August 1976 and my mother took him home with her on November 1976 and Manny Boy was entrusted to a babysitter while they worked.

I arrived in New York December 28, 1976 and after settling down I called Fatima. Her voice sounded great as we spoke about my new life with Lee. Then it changed to a more somber tone as she told me that in early December she had gone to her gynecologist as she felt lumps in her breast. Her doctor told her they were only milk ducts that had settled since she had stopped breast feeding. She gave her some pills to take and she went home. After two weeks, the lumps were still there and this time pain accompanied the touch. So she decided to consult with another doctor who immediately did a biopsy. The results were thunderous. Fatima was misdiagnosed the first time and now she had a malignant breast cancer. The doctor without wasting any time ordered a mastectomy and it was done within a few days time. It was not the best news to receive as we faced the New Year but it was more devastating to hear her voice, so burdened with sadness as her marriage started to whither and die.

Thanksgiving 1977, Fatima called me crying hysterically. She said that her husband wanted to leave and have dinner with their son's babysitter. He was also taking Manny Boy with him. I wanted to kill him! How can he be so cruel to her knowing she had cancer. How could he not wait until she was no longer around before he started this affair with the babysitter? We knew it all along and so did my sister. She started suspecting something was going on when Manny Boy came home with new toys that Harriet bought him and when her husband came home late whenever he could. She said she called the cops when he pushed her and slapped her face. It was reported as domestic violence but there wasn't anything the cops could do. He left that night alone and did not return until the wee hours of the morning. My sister's love for this man was beyond her life so she lived with it and still pined for the simple gesture of affection he could give her.

## "Pride is spiritual cancer. It eats the very possibility of love or contentment, or even common sense". C.S. Lewis

Is this the measure of true love? I thought marriage was about two people who vowed to be one with each other, being faithful, being loyal and most of all not wanting to be with someone else. I tried to understand why he went in that direction. My sister wore a wig when her hair started to fall off so he would still find her attractive but what they did in the privacy of their home was something I dared not tread but realistically I knew why and just like every storm in a relationship, that too passed but the eye of the storm remained intact and had enticed the man my sister loved deeply. She was willing to take that just so he would still be around as he chose to.

After that extremely emotional outburst, my sister called me in January to tell me that her doctor found tumors on her neck. I immediately thought silently "Oh my God, the cancer cells are moving to her head". As always I tried not to show signs of panic for I needed to be strong for her but we cried over the phone knowing there was a bigger storm ahead of her. So she went through another chemo treatment and we all continued on with our lives. Without her telling me I knew that their relationships had remained the same and expectations had become a thing of the past.

In March 1978, Fatima was admitted to the hospital. Her chemotherapy treatment was giving her some side effects that basically immobilized her.. So a new drug was introduced. It was better but it promised nothing, just like all the others that they experimented on her. It was really just a guessing game and she had no choice but to play along.

Summer 1978 in New York was beautiful and Lee was scheduled to leave for his business trip and thoughts of my going with him were discussed and I was in heaven. I would get to hug and kiss my babies again! Maybe this time I can bring them with me. Oh, God, that would be incredibly wonderful. I could not wait to finalize our travel plans. Then I got a call from my sister's husband. Fatima was back in the hospital again. This was in late May 1978. He said "I know you do not want to even talk to me but I have to tell you that Fatima is not doing well. She is asking for you". My heart sunk and so did my chance to hug my children for the moment. But I had another mission, one that could not wait, one that is between life and death.

One of the many wonderful things in my marriage to Lee was the opportunity to travel and go places with him on his business trips and with my children so far away, I needed to divert my ongoing loneliness for them so when Lee told me of the business convention in Georgia, my heart was lifted from the sadness that had burdened it. It was in the late May 1978 when we flew to Georgia and I had busied myself assisting him during the convention and enjoying the warmth of his love and total caring and attentiveness towards me.

Each night as I cuddle next to him my world seemed to change to total calmness even though thoughts of my sister Fatima would cross my mind and a flash of worry pinched my heart a bit. I had learned too soon that there are things that one cannot brush aside and even a temporary change of my state of mind cannot remove that striking fear of her terminality and the thought of her passing at such a young age.

It was at the airport in Georgia when Lee and I said our goodbyes. He made sure my flight to Chicago left first before he boarded on his to New York. So I flew to Chicago with a heavy heart not knowing what this trip would offer me and what my leaving my beloved husband would mean to him. He understood the need for me to be there and he gave me his blessings. It was basically me in turmoil inside. I was torn between two important people in my life. It was summer of 1978. Though it was hot, my body felt coldness with the underlying truth before me.

I was met at the airport by Fatee's husband Emmanuel. We were cordial and spoke mostly about my sister's present condition and what was ahead of us. First stop was at the hospital where fatigue and emotional distress had been put aside and the excitement of seeing her was all that was in my heart. She was asleep when we walked in and I quietly moved closer to her bedside and put my hand over her so badly colored arms from the daily injections and drawing of blood. She stirred and as she opened her eyes I saw a smile in them and then she said "I am so glad you are here". I was too. Then she asked me where Ludette was and I told her she would be coming as soon as she had taken care of things in New York. She smiled with a hopeful sigh, knowing us three would be together again!

I did not stay long for I was very tired and she understood. She knew she would see me again in the morning. Sleep came fast that night. I emptied my emotional bucket to make room for new ones that I knew would fill it up very quickly. My thoughts were there with my sister and the questions in my head. I was sure they would be answered as the days go by. But first, I must tend to Fatee and give her all the best of me.

Everyday was spent at the hospital. Sometimes I would take a cab back to the house just to get a break and at times to cook a certain dish she would request which always gave me hope that she was getting better. But when she would only take two or three spoonful of the food and could not eat anymore my heart sunk a little each time. With the help of the nurse we would attempt to walk her but she was too weak to even get her out of the bed so we gave up on that. We talked a lot mostly centered towards her husband and sons, especially Jong-Jong who she had not seen since he was taken to the Philippines by my mother in November 1976. She longed for him and wanted to see him. I could not tell her that she would never see her baby boy again because discussions made by those who were caring for him believed it was best for Jong-Jong not to see his mother that way. No one thought what that would do for Fatee. They were more concerned with the effect it would have with a toddler than what it would have with a dying mother.

**"In life, there are moments when you miss someone so much that you feel like you could only fully live by holding that person tight in your arms"**

With her beautiful long black hair now gone, Fatee had lost all her desires to wear a wig. But she did not need one for she was still as pretty as she was in spite of the little loss of muscles in her left cheek that caused it to sag a bit. Looking back now I believe she could have had a mild stroke that was not detected or suspected and with everything she had gone through, this was not far from it! My little sister, the quiet one, the gentle one who would not harm anyone yet this giant monster called cancer had taken away every dream, every hope, every peace from her and most of all it had taken her away from her two sons.

My stay in Chicago became routine. Every morning I would take care of my nephew Manny Boy before he went to Day Care. Then after I ate my breakfast I would hail a cab to the hospital where I would stay until her husband arrived from work or after picking up Manny Boy from the sitter. Often times Fatima would ask me "Where is Manny?" and I would have no answer but "he should be here soon" even though I knew where he was.

The drugs and pain killers they were giving her made her sleep most of the time and much as I would liked her to be awake, in my mind I thought it best she slept so she did not have time to think things over that could emotionally hurt her. I believed she knew that her husband was having an affair but she was now too weak to argue. All she wanted was to see him, be with him and die with him in the room. She was very smart that she opted not to ask because she no longer wanted to waste her time on situations she could not change, fix and most of all carry in her heart.

Lee called me everyday, always concerned for my well being. He even called the hospital Administrator who he knew because of our nursing business and requested a bed for me as I had sometimes had to sleep on two chairs that I would connect. There were days when my sadness would overcome me and as soon as she had fallen asleep I would tell the nurse's station that I would be going to the roof top. Here is where I wrote my journal. Here is where I cried. Here is where I allowed myself to miss Lee so much. Here is where I yearned for my children whose absence made my heart hollow and hungry for their innocence and trust in me. Here is where I could have my private conversation with God ... a long conversation of merciful pleading.

Finally Ludette arrived and it was almost like a load was taken off me. I wanted Fatima to see her and feel her concern and love. I wanted to see her make our sister laugh and she did. But behind Ludette's laughter was sadness. She was shocked to see Fatima's condition yet she never gave her any reason to believe that her end was coming. Alone and back in the house, we shared our fears and we faced reality and we hurt.

Ludette's arrival was a blessing to me for I no longer carried the fully loaded emotional bucket on my shoulder alone, When they were small, they fought a lot and I was the referee but their fights did not last long for both had enough love for each other to ignore the contest of power that emerges between them. Being the youngest, Ludette was quite spoiled and in her mischievous ways, she gave us reasons to stay away from her but she had the quality of persistence and knew how to deliver annoyance! Now, Fatima was laying there, so helpless, no energy to argue, no room for anger., no desire to renew their childhood power games. No time.

Between watching Fatima at the hospital, Ludette also needed time to look for a job. She went to Illinois to settle down, perhaps in her mind, to be near Fatima as she had no idea how serious her condition had gotten. She had no clue that her coming to Illinois was just to say goodbye to a sister she fought with and she loved in a way that sisters do. I was glad she was preparing herself for a new life and a new beginning in a city she thought would bring happy times with Fatima, not in a funeral procession that was soon coming.

On the second month I was there, we noticed that her husband was taking advantage of our presence and would show up at the hospital quite late. We never left the hospital until he came as we knew Fatima would become restless and at this point we were bent into making sure her emotional state of mind was steady although we knew we had no control over her longing heart. On week-ends he always had something to do and we kept Fatima company, ready to say assuring things when her husband failed to show up.

Unfortunately for Manny, he did not realize he was dealing with two very smart, over-thinking women whose intuitions and gut feelings were almost always true. So the few week-ends before Fatima passed away, we made plans to be gone the whole day and only stopped by the hospital in the evening. Those few week-ends her husband was at the hospital became a source of smiles and simple contentment. She was happy, very happy! How he felt, it did not matter to us.

## "Love is still the most poignant and powerful force in the world"

One morning we overheard Manny over the phone as he was talking to his mother who was at that time in the Philippines caring for their younger son Joseph (Jong-Jong) since he was brought home by my mother in November 1976. He was very nasty as he shared with his mom his dislike for us and not wanting us around the house and that he preferred to have our older sister Vilma over us. We were furious! As soon as he got off the phone I asked him to sit with us in the kitchen as we needed to talk.

I told him we overheard his conversation with his mother and that it did not sit well with us and so this talk was necessary. I said: "The three of us are all here for one reason ..Fatima. It does not matter to us whether you like us or not. It does not matter to us what you do when this is all over but it matters to us what you do when our sister is there laying down in her death bed. We are not here for you and we understand where we stand and we are not playing your game! We have to focus all our time and attention for Fatima because she will not be here with us much longer". No apologies, no crying, screaming, no arguing. It was almost a one way street conversation and my sister Ludette and I were the driver of one powerful vehicle.

While the end of our conversation was simple silence, I knew that our message was delivered well and we no longer have to pretend that we are family but rather three people going in one direction yet not aware of what lies ahead. I have taken the role of a big sister here and I have proven to him that blood is thicker than water, especially if the water is running down in a wasteful way.

Every single day that the Lord has made, I pined and hoped for a miraculous recovery which grew dimmer everyday. Fatima had no desire to eat and if she craved something special, I would go home and make it for her only to feel sadder as I watched her take two to three spoonful and then give up and just lies there quietly I could almost hear her mind!

I have witnessed so many times how the nurse would turn her sideways and I always felt a pang in my stomach as I gazed at her black and blue back from all the needles that had penetrated her now very skinny body. She confessed to me one morning how a particular oriental nurse would hurt her so badly when she was drawing blood from her. She said she would raise her hand high enough and then throws the needle like a dart deep into her already very sensitive skin. Sure enough as she was telling me this the same nurse walked in, syringe in hand and without a word, raised Fatima's gown and her target was hit with Fatima screaming!

As soon as she was done, I went to the Nurse's station and told the Supervisor not to let that nurse near my sister ever again and that was the last time we had seen her. The drawing of blood samples continued forever until I could not stand it anymore so I spoke with my sister's doctor and asked him why they keep drawing blood and he said "we need to know the count" and I said "for what?". Why is it necessary to keep poking her when we know it is just a matter of time? Why is she being tortured when she should be left alone to have a peaceful sleep? It is that necessary? So the drawing of blood lessened and I no longer saw agitation and heard no more screaming. Finally, my sister was left alone and her body was respected and cared for in a kinder way. Finally, she no longer had to fight the fear of being poked, more so, the physical torture of her now so weak body!

Day in and day out I watched my sweet sister deteriorate. It was almost like waiting for the Prince of Death to show up and there was nothing I could do to stop him from seizing the life of my sister, a life she devoted to just loving the man she loved beyond herself. Deep inside me, I did not want to witness any more suffering, physically and emotionally yet I clung to the very tip of hope that a miracle would happen and all that was happening before my eyes would be like a dream! But that was not to be so. Her journey may not even reach around the bend where all hopes and wishes may just be a few more steps away. Her broken heart could never be mended again!

The fearful day came. Her doctor wanted to talk with me. I stepped out of the room and sat with her doctor as he in his softest voice said to me "I am so sorry but the latest lab test had shown her cancer had spread to her liver". My brain was saying "what does it mean?" yet my mouth uttered "is she going to die soon?" words my ears did not want to hear! He said there is no telling when it will eventually happen but the cancer had been very aggressive and because of her weakened state of being was way down low, internally, there were no more soldiers to fight the battle.

As we parted he said to me "If all possible, make all that she desires come true". In other words give her reasons to be happy even for a short while and I knew what those desires were, yet I had no control over them. Without her speaking it out loud, I knew she longed to have her husband by her side every waking moment and to have her youngest boy Jong-Jong back in Illinois to hug him with all her might and never let go of him ever again!

As soon as I stepped into her room she asked me what the doctor had to say. For a brief moment I was silent, wondering what was the wisest thing to do. I did not want to cause more sadness yet I did not want to lie. Here she was, slowly dying right before my eyes, how could I deceive her? How can I be like her deceiving husband? I decided to tell her the truth.

What she asked me next were thunderous to my ears. "Am I going to die?" I held her thin and blotched hand gently and leaned over her bed railing and with controlled voice I said "Your doctor did not say that Fatee. Only God can determine that and for as long as He has not come for you, we shall continue to hope and never give up". Then another deafening words were uttered as though in mere acceptance "Mars, please watch over my boys. I want the house I bought through my work at the bank to go through." Saddened by this I asked "you still want that house even though there is no assurance you will be there?" and her loving reply choked me up "That house is theirs. I want my sons to have a home". Not only did I assure her I would watch them, I also made a promise!

Sometime in the later part of August 1978, she begged her doctor to release her and send her home. We sat in conference with the doctor, trying to understand every aspect of her leaving the hospital where she was receiving total care. Her doctor told us that my sister was on her last journey and want to be in the comfort of her own home. We had very strict instructions to follow and were assured that any slight concern should be relayed to the hospital staff. Immediately. My sister was on an alert case.

The day came and she was brought home. For some reason or so, I cannot seem to recall if we took her home or if the ambulance did. One thing I knew for sure was she lived on the third floor of an apartment complex with no elevator service. Her weakened body could not make those steps so the only solution was for her husband to carry her all the way up! For that short moment, Fatee was happy not only because she was home but because after all those months of her husbands infidelity, she was void of that body closeness she longed for. Two years before she was diagnosed with breast cancer, her husband had begun his affair with the babysitter. Prior to that he was already playing the ladies man! Many nights she wondered in whose body her husband was laying next to. A very long nightmare!

Now she was home and longed to be cuddled but those precious moments were short lived. For three nights she kicked and screamed and cried. My sister Ludette and I jumped up from our sleep and be by her side to calm her down. Her husband did the same. She told us that there were witches at the foot of her bed, pulling her legs! We would sit by her bed until she finally dozed off into oblivion, tired and frightened and delirious.

For three days and night, I held both her hands as we walked towards the bathroom. She was taking baby steps, wobbly and unsure. One time she lifted her top to show me the scar from her mastectomy. I cringed at the sight, I cried at the thought. I criticized quietly for a bad job the surgeon did on my sister's cancerous breast. No woman would feel any better with that terrible pancake like surgery they did on her. But my face showed no sign of how I felt. I could not for I needed to remain strong for my sister. She needed my strength!

## "Nothing is so strong as gentleness. Nothing is so gentle as real strength" (St. Francis de Salas )

The next day I called her doctor and shared with him the episodes that had been happening and he advised us to bring her back to the hospital so proper medication could be administered. So on the fourth day of her release from the hospital, we took her back. To this day I cannot seem to recall if we took her ourselves after her husband arrived from work or if we sent for an ambulance. I guess this was nothing worth remembering for our main concern was her. I could not have taken her myself but the moment we brought her back to the hospital, it became clear to me that there will be no more chance left that would allow her to step inside her home again. That was her last visit. Her real home was being prepared by the One who created her, the One who loved her unconditionally, and was now coming to usher her home!

On August 26, 1978, the three of us sat around her hospital bed, hardly a word was said as we watched her slowly slipping into her world of oblivion. She was very calm now. A few hours that day as she writhed in pain, I spoke to her doctor asking him to ease her pain and he told me that he needed her husband's permission to do that. Firmly and decidedly I reminded her doctor that I was family and family comes first in situations like this plus there was no way I would wait any longer until her husband had returned from work or from his mistress's house. I had to take over. I was not going to let her suffer much longer so I insisted that her morphine dosage be increased and to that her doctor gave in but with the truth that she may never wake up. "Wake Up To What?" my mind was shouting it out!

A few minutes later the nurse came in and I watched her inject a liquid into another bag that was flowing life supporting substance into my sister's now so weak body. She stopped writhing and even moaning. She became calm and all I could see was her very slow breathing and her skinny body that was almost swallowed by her railed bed. I was there. I was ready to part with my sister, the one who I wished was rewarded with a good life for being one of my father's Courageous Daughter! Yes, that is what my dad called us three for we dared to venture away from home, away from the security of loving parents, away from the land where we were born and away from the life we had known. Each one of us had a story to tell but not as tragic as Fatima's life story and to think her Catholic name was "Fatima Victoria". Victory in its ironic form perhaps.

My sister Ludette was sitting at the foot of her bed, her husband on the left side, stroking her black and blue hand and I was sitting by her right side, stroking her needle-poked arm, my head bowed in prayers. Suddenly Ludette called my name and said "Mars, Fatee is not breathing!". We both stood up and turned to her and I looked at her stomach and I knew her sacrifices were over and we cried.

All those months of putting up a front of strength were gone. I did not have to pretend anymore. I sobbed violently and hurtingly, my hand still holding her still warm arms. Her husband came over to me and put his arms around my shoulders to control my body from shaking. It felt like all the pain she had endured came passing through me as I cried like I never cried before. Soon the room was filled with hospital staff and all I could hear was her name echoeing around the room and in my head.

When they were done removing all the attachments from her body, they left us to be alone with her. I walked quietly as if not to wake a sleeping baby, to the side of her bed and I reached for her head and gently caressed it as I said my goodbye. As I looked at her now peaceful face, what I saw was the ultimate blow to my aching heart. At the corner of her left eye were tears that gathered but did not fall. Were they tears of joy for she had met her Creator? Were they tears of joy for she had met my parents, grandparents, brothers, and her sister? Or were they tears of sadness for leaving us? I thought they were like crystals, clear and sparkling, like the life she was about to have in her eternal home.

After the funeral, her husband invited us to see Fatee's dream house for her family. I did not say a word and sat silently, lost in my own world of relief. Riding in the limousine were my older sister Vilma and youngest sister Ludette and when we arrived at the house they all got out of the car and I refused to go with them. I said with bitterness "This is not Fatee's house and will never be ". I sat in the car filled with hatred, anger and disgust for the man my sister loved to death and who seemed to be unaffected by her passing. There was not a tinge of sadness in his face but smiles that I read to say "I am free".

I stayed for another week in Chicago to spend some time with my two sisters but more than that I wanted to make sure that before I left Ludette would have settled down in her one room apartment above the house of an Armenian family. It really was very cute and the furnitures she had all came from "slightly used stores". I just lost my younger sister Fatee and now here I am again, worrying over my youngest sister Ludette. I dreaded leaving her there but I had to get back to New York. I consoled myself with the fact that she was pretty strong, resourceful and gutsy enough to venture in another place where she knew nobody except our brother-in-law who she now also hated!

We had a great whole week ... lots of laughter, lots of family memories brought to light and lots of reliefs knowing Fatee was no longer suffering physically and emotionally. She was safe now. I flew back to the waiting arms of my wonderful husband Lee Perry Kramer. It was a very eventful coming home for me because two weeks earlier Lee threw his last pack of cigarettes at the Philippine International Airport on his way back to New York. It was both an exciting reunion being away for so long and with tragedy behind us.

As if there was a divine intervention, Lee's friend from Ireland who was running a Travel Agency extended an invitation for us to go there with a great possibility of a business partnership. Soon after we received our plane tickets we were on our way to Ireland in November 1978, almost a perfect time to go away and be happy for a change.

When we arrived in Ireland, we rented a car. Simple right? Not really. As soon as we got the car we started laughing because the steering wheel is on the right side and when we have to make a right turn, we have to go to the left lanes! Lee made several mistakes which ended up with us hysterically laughing especially when he turned the wipers on and it was not even raining! We drove through the towns of Ireland enjoying the sight of horse-drawn milk-carrying carriages, open fields with bundles of hay and homes with roofs that were thatched and so neat.

We had dinner at the Bunratty Castle, entertained by the local musicians and dancers and our food were served medieval times with wooden soup bowls, wooden forks and spoons, wooden plates, and then breaking bread with our bare hands. While this experience may be common in other places the difference was that we were in an actual castle. One of the things I have heard about Ireland is the very famous Blarney Stone Castle. I was told that if I kissed the Blarney Stone, I would have the Gift of Gab so I was determined to do just that, after all, I have been quite a shy one and a little help can do me good.

So to test this, Lee and I braved the steep, narrow and dark spiral stairs of the castle which was now basically a skeleton castle with just the walls and floors framing it. Carelessness can make you drop down with nothing to catch you but the main floor where people were walking around and trying to compact memories in their cameras. An older gentleman was waiting for me to kneel down, position myself to lean backwards, just holding on to dear life as he held both my legs and helped me eased my way under the kissing stone wall. It was scary but I was determined to experience a life-changing part of my journey. For ten glorious days we were alive again. We were together and we were in a foreign country having the time of our lives. Pretty soon our vacation was over but a new business partnership was in the making.

Just a few days after we were back home, Lee received a telefax message from his office in Manila advising him that his Filipino business partner Johnny Limjuco had a heart attack and was gone. Just like that! They were not just business partners, they were like brothers. Sadness took over our lives again which certainly affected Lee more than me. Lee was a family to the Limjucos and he loved everyone of them. For many years he had gone there on a quarterly basis and it was always a great trip for both of them. Lee buried himself with work and his loss remained entombed in his broken heart. Lee had a very soft side about him and his silence only meant that he was grieving inside. When I would take his hand, he would look at me with the saddest eyes where tears starts to swell up and no words are spoken but a simple mutual understanding of the pain that comes with a great loss.

About a month or so later, Lee received a message from Ireland that his friend and future business partner Noel Martin had a massive heart attack while swimming. There were no words to utter but he called Noel's fiancee to offer his condolences. Was our memorable trip to Ireland Noel's parting gift to us? Why did this sweet and gentle friend depart so soon and in the manner he went? No one had an answer and once more Lee's heart was shuttered and pained.

For some very strange reasons, Lee's parents, Mildred Brown Kramer and Stanley Kramer decided not to fly to New York for the holidays. I spoke with my darling mother-in-law and she was so upset that Stanley decided not to go to New York. Angry and sad and deeply disappointed, she told me "the next time I come to New York I would be in a box!" I wished I had intervened but I thought it was more of Lee's place to talk with his dad. So for the first time since I married to Lee's family, we did not have them at our home for the holidays even though they did not celebrate Christmas. All that my mother-in-law wanted was to be with her son Lee, the love of her life.

Soon as the New Year ushered in, all I needed was to wait one more day and it was my birthday and Lee had not told me his plans and I was just leaving it up to him for he knew how to dote on me. Besides I wanted to be surprised by my Knight in Shining Armor who adored me from head to toe!

Each year since we met, he had always done his best to make my birthday truly special because I was away from home and my son Tyrone and daughter Mia who I longed for every single day. He knew what to do to fill that void and to fill it with his own special love for me. So I waited for the day!

In the morning of January 2, 1979, we got a call from Tennessee, from Lee's dad hysterically crying as he told Lee his mother had a stroke and was at the hospital. For whatever reason there was that compelled us to drive to this day remains a mystery to me. Why did we not fly? Why did we not consider the length of driving time we would do when we were so much in a hurry to get there and be with the special woman Lee and I both adored and loved. The only thing I could think of now is we were perhaps so shocked with the news and our first instinct was to get in our car and get there! We just pack initial things we needed and tried not to waste even a single minute. It took us seventeen stressful hours when we could have flown for a couple of hours. Bad decision but it was too late to make any changes. If only she would hold on and waited for us. I prayed.

The sight of new snow on the ground and on the trees was breathtaking and it helped me ease my worried head yet there in the midst of all the beauty of mother nature, was my mother-in-law's sweet face, the tiny Jewish mother whose entire love in her heart was meant for Lee. She was getting mad at Stanley who refused to stop working even though he was already 75 years old. All Mildred wanted to do with the remaining years of her life was to move to New York and be with Lee and her three grandchildren. But Stanley was a man who only thought of himself and her admonition to sell their home in Tennessee and move to New York fell on deaf ears and Mildred wallowed in her sorrow.

Lee must have been over speeding throughout the trip but that did not bring us closer enough to be able to say goodbye to my dear Mildred. She could not wait for us anymore. She was no longer in her room when we arrived and we wanted to see her wherever she was but to no avail. The hospital staff could not see how broken our hearts were. So now when I think of her, I only see the liveliness of her being, the gentleness of her touches and the unquestionable love she had for Lee and her unconditional acceptance of a daughter-in-law who was a gentile.

We shared a unique thing: our initials. MBK – Mildred Brown Kramer and Marcia Bundalian Kramer. I even found a purse that had our initials and I used that purse until it served me well. She did passed away January 2nd and my birthday is January 3rd. Lee and I were married March 9th and her birthday was March 10th. But most important of all is we had a common love: Lee Perry Kramer!

Following her Jewish tradition of being laid to rest the next day, arrangements were made and we went to bed. Exhaustion both body, mind and heart was enough to knock us down fast and we had to leave in the wee hours of the morning in time to be in New York when her remains arrived. Lee's children took the responsibilities of making funeral arrangements there. Stanley flew with her casket.

As we drove back home, we were lost perhaps in our own world of just rewinding the fond memories of one of the greatest mother in the world. Oblivious to his driving, Lee got a speeding ticket, to our surprise of course but we did not even talk about it and instead we just held hands and allowed that silent grief to take over us. Mom was in our thoughts and hearts and was now gone.

On the horizon, the sun was peeking through. It was a beautiful cold morning, Lee pulled over a rest area and we both got out to stretch our tired bodies. It was colder than I expected but Lee put his loving arms around me, pulled me closer towards him and held me tight. I felt so secure in his arms. Then he spoke: "I am so sorry Angel but this is not how I wanted to celebrate your birthday. I just did not want you to think I did not remember" and with that he put his hand inside his coat and pulled out a small box. Then he said "This is not the way I wanted to give this to you. Just know I love you very much".

I slowly opened the box and there it was ... the most beautiful ruby ring I ever saw. It was pear cut with diamonds and ruby. It looked so expensive I was reluctant to put it on and when I did, I felt I was the luckiest wife in the world. Here was my husband who just lost his mother and he not only remembered my birthday he did not forget to bring his present in our haste to leave for Tennessee. Tears of joy had temporarily replaced the tears of sorrow that came to us so suddenly. I do not recall how long we stood there, locked in tender embrace, in the middle of nowhere with snow in its purest, surrounding us with peace and quiet where only our heartbeats could be heard and our love for each other kept us warm and safe. It was a moment to treasure, to put in the chamber of my heart and lock it just as I have put Lee in my life, to cherish and to hold, to love always, in sickness and in good health, for richer or poorer, till death do us part!

Everyone came to our apartment after her internment. It felt so different not having Mildred at a family gathering. She would have loved being there with the people she loved. Now everyone was there who loved her. That night I told Lee what his mom said to me about her coming back to New York in a box. He felt so sad and so bad knowing how unhappy she was all these years, home alone all day while her husband worked until he was forced to finally retire. By then it was too late to make a move, by then her eyes could no longer cry tears, they have dried up from years of crying herself to sleep. Now all our lives have been altered and all will not be the same but we all must move on.

Being together at the office and at home, 24/7 was not really the best situation in a marriage and we were finding less quality time when we got home. Just gotten tired of the routine and we brought home any issues from work. So Lee thought of starting a business for me and he spoke to his dad about it and he agreed it was a good idea. So we spent our week-ends looking for a possible area with a vacant store. We found one on Northern Boulevard in Flushing. The size of the store was big enough for our intended stock and the display window was perfect. The one thing I was not crazy about was at the back there was still traces of burned walls and I could also smell it. So the owners agreed to replace the damaged walls and got it painted. In February 1979, we had our Grand Opening as I stared proudly at the name of my store: "Marcee's of Manila".

It was intended to be a low-cost T-shirt store but having seen better quality and brand names at the garment center in Manhattan changed all that. What was to be a plain shirt-shop became a boutique. Things were good after the Grand Opening. Lee and I only had one car so he would drop me off at the store and then pick me up after work. Things started to change for the better although I still asked him about the business. This was my way of finding out how his day went and therefore I would know how to adjust to his mood which was seldom not good. Lee was a very happy guy who just loved to tell jokes or just teases me to make me laugh.

The best part of our day was after dinner when we would sit up in bed and watched TV and enjoyed each other's company especially when we are holding hands or just cuddling. Even from the first time I met him he looked like a tower of strength. When we walked he would always take my hand and hold it firmly, securely and it felt so wonderful. When I nestled my head on his chest and his hands are caressing my back with such tenderness, and then kisses my head, I sometimes fall asleep with such contentment and he would not move a bit even if he needed to.

Looking back now, I begin to recall all the sadness that knocked on our door. One more sadness came to us in a manner that is unbelievable. The event at our store is now rewinding in my mind. Fall, 1979. One Saturday night as we were asleep, the phone rang. And I picked up the receiver and with some sort of hesitation, I said "hello". Calls at this late is always a fearful one for there is always a possibility of bad news that usually come from family members. But this time it was not. It was the automatic alert message system we had installed at the store. My heart jump as I heard "Robbery in Progress" at our store. Lee was already half awake. His daughter Randy also got the message which prompted a call to us, Her husband Lowell and Lee drove to the store and when they got there the police were already checking the area. Nothing. Lee opened the store and they all went in and looked around but did not see anything suspicious.. It was a false alarm.

Behind the store was a railroad track that rattled the store when the train passed. Thinking that the alarm was most likely triggered by the train, everyone left with Lee and Lowell eager to get back to bed. At 2:00 in the morning, our phone rang again, with the same message so Lee and Lowell drove back to the store, looked around and saw nothing. This time the police came later. Fearing that the next alarm would already cost us money for the police to be there, Lee decided to turn off the alarm, shut all the lights, locked the door and hurried to the car for this time it was already very cold. Finally, he thought "no more disturbances, finally peace and quiet. He discussed with Lowell of changing the alarm system into a better one that is not too sensitive. He just was not about to go through this hassle again! One night was all he could take.

Sunday morning we left Bayside at 9:00 and drove to the garment industry in Manhattan and bought more than what we always did. We were excited to show new merchandise. On our way back, Lee asked me where I would like to price tag the garments and being Sunday, I chose our apartment. So we stopped by the store and from the look outside, one would not even suspect the chaos that we had to go through Saturday night. Lee parked the car in front of the store and went in to get my tool. As quickly as he walked in, he was out, his face was pale and his mouth wide open! Then he said to me "Angel, let us just close the shop, come with me and you will know why". With his strong arms on my shoulder, he held me close as he opened the door.

Only one emotion surfaced in my brain ~ Shocked! On the floor were empty hangers, clothes everywhere, my designer jeans all gone! The entire store was ransacked and only the valuable clothes were taken. As we slowly stepped around clothes that were sprawled on the floor, we moved to the back room where we found more less expensive clothing. We checked the back door and it was still locked. We looked at each other and almost simultaneously looked up the ceiling and there right above us was a big square hole that was sawed enough for an adult to go through and pass the clothing over to the other person on the rooftop. This gave me chills. It really felt we were violated. Could they have been at the rooftop when Lee and Lowell and the cops were there? Did the cops even check the roof? I do not recall asking Lee this when he first responded to the alarm.

Soon the cops arrived. They did the whole procedure and as days passed, they had nothing for us to smile about. We were a small store and they would not get much from us so there was no motivation for them to pursue the matter. Whoever burglarized our store were pretty smart as fingerprints were nowhere to be found, so the cops said. There was no lead … not one!

We were left with no choice but to close the store. It did not even have a chance to grow. And our inventory showed we would be in the hole for at least $20,000 and to stay in business after being wiped out would mean more financial loss for us not just having to dole out more money for the clothes but also comes other expenses. So we put up signs at the store window that we were closing and everything in the store was discounted. We just wanted everything gone so we could walk out of the door and forget the Nightmare on Northern Boulevard and make time for ourselves!

The holidays came and went and we spent it with a good amount of sadness, each one opting not to discuss the short-lived business venture my loving Lee wanted for me. We mostly talked about the coming New Year and plans we were making but most of all no more tragedies!

January 1980 ~ Early morning. Lee went to the bathroom and I heard him call me over in a very frantic voice. Stumbling from the bed he put his arms around me and pointed at the toilet bowl. I could not believe my eyes! The water was all red! He had urinated blood! All I heard was my voice saying "Oh my God!" as total fear enveloped our being. We waited a few hours to call Dr. Weinstock and as soon as he heard what happened he immediately took us in. Lab test were done and to our relief he told us the urine test showed normal but he asked Lee to see him again as soon as he got back from his trip to the Philippines to interview more nurses. Lee had no discomfort whatsoever so he proceeded with his planned two weeks trip.

Lee came back loaded with files and paperwork and he buried his head with all the business his trip had blessed him. He was a workaholic and had so much drive that weeks went by and he did not see Dr. Weinstock again. He did not urinate blood again! Immediate concern was simply brushed aside.

Other than quitting smoking, cold turkey, on August 1978, Lee pretty much maintained his daily routine and always managed to be happy. He was a very witty man with a great sense of humor. One thing I have heard too many times "Marry someone who can make you laugh" and that he did more so when he would find me looking out the window at dusk with a longing for my children written all over my face. He would go behind my back and puts his so assuring arms around my neck, kisses my head and then say something funny and he would always end that with a huge bear hug that made me feel so loved and secure. Lee was my morning sunshine and he was my star at night!

Looking back now, I remember him coming back with a cough from his last trip to Manila. That worsened and it became a concern, a reason for us to see our family doctor, Dr. Weinstock, a gentle doctor and a very kind one as well. I was sitting in the examination room when Dr. Weinstock asked him to repeat "99" many times to the point it sounded so funny to me that I started to giggle and next thing, Lee was laughing and so was the doctor.

The doctor wanted to be certain of something so he ordered for chest x-ray that would be done at 1:30 in the afternoon so we went home and had lunch and he left. I had to stay home as the furniture of the kids were being delivered in time for their arrival in New York in Spring. Half of my heart was rejoicing and the other half was fearing for inside my mind, I could still see that toiled bowl filled with blood and now he was coughing and worst, an x-ray was ordered.

Lee came home about three in the afternoon like nothing was troubling him. He was hungry and changed and prepared pickled herrings with crackers for us while I was in the bedroom taking care of things. I asked him for the results of his test and he said Dr. Weinstock was going to call him later so we went about our chores and waited. He remained in the kitchen getting ready to make dinner for us. He loved to cook but he would go crazy with the Filipino dishes I cooked for him!

At about 4:00 pm the phone rang. He did not pick it up so I did. To this day I can still hear the voice of Dr. Weinstock and what he said to me: "Marcia, this is Dr. Weinstock. Where is Lee? (In the kitchen I answered). Can he hear you? ( No, was my reply as I was still in the bedroom ).You are his wife and you need to know the truth. It does not look good. (What do you mean? I asked). His lungs are in pretty bad shape. (Does he know I asked) No, was his reply. Dr. Weinstock said he told him that he might have caught tuberculosis in the Philippines while he was there. "But it does not look good Marcia and I am very sorry" was his last words.

I put down the phone very slowly as if I had done something wrong and did not want to get caught. Dr. Weinstock's words screaming in my ears. I look out of the bedroom door and saw Lee still busy in the kitchen. My heart sunk at the sight of the man I loved who did not know he had just been diagnosed with a mighty strong, terribly scary challenge called Cancer.

Too busy to be too concerned, Lee worked like nothing was wrong in his world and I played along, hoping it would be TB just as Dr. W.eintock lied to him. Looking at Lee, one would not be able to tell that something more eminent and devastating was in the making.

One morning, as he was getting ready for work, he called me into the bathroom and showed me a red mole on his head. He said he was combing his hair a few days ago and scratched what he thought was a pimple which bled at that time but he did not think nothing of it. Within that few days, that "pimple" had grown to the size of a very red cherry.

Not taking any chances, we went to see Dr. Weinstock who recommended a dermatologist in Manhattan. We immediately were seen and as I sat at the doctor's office, I could see across the hallway Lee being examined. When he came back to the doctor's office with a bandage on the area where the growth was, we sat there, holding hands, waiting for the doctor to give us some good news. There I saw in Lee's eyes, a very concerned look and in the way he held my hand. The fear he felt came rushing through my vein as I begun feeling his hand tighter on mine. I had the same fear because I already knew.

Finally the doctor came, sat behind his desk and with the coldest voice I have ever heard he said: "You have cancer and it has metastasized and it is un-operable. You just have to go home and take care of your business and be prepared." I could not say anything nor did I scream at the doctor or cry. All I saw was Lee's two hands holding on to the armchairs, red from the tight grip and his nails ready to sink in the chair padding. The doctor was brief and so insensitive to Lee and I was mad for the way he blurted out the bad news!

As we walked out of the hospital, I told him we needed a second opinion or even a third and he agreed with me. It was early February and winter was cold but we were warm as we walked hand in hand, glove to glove, hoping for the best, hoping the doctor was wrong.

We saw two more doctors – the last one we saw on February 14, 1980. He was a much older man who was very kind and very sensitive to Lee. He told us that there was a new chemotheraphy drug that he would like to try with Lee, but only giving him just 20% chance of remission. Finally, there was a glimmer of hope in our hearts especially when he wanted to start right away.

On our way out of the building and as we crossed the street, hand in hand, we had a different gait. We were so happy. Lee wanted to stop at the flower shop to celebrate and we ended up with some branches of pussy willows. I did not think of it then but now that I have gone back to the past, it just occurred to me "why a willow"? Willows are sad looking trees, they droop and hang and are reaching towards the ground unlike other trees that lift their bodies towards the sky. There is even one called a Weeping Willow. I remember one winter day we were on the road and we passed a lake that had froze and at the bank were weeping willow trees, very green but hanging like they had no strength. I asked Lee why they are called weeping willow and he said "I would be weeping too if I am out there in this freezing winter!" Yes, that was Lee .... my lung exerciser, my joker, my warmth during the winter and my sunshine on a gloomy day. I miss him so.

So Lee's treatment begun. I drove him to Sloan Kettering in Manhattan, dropped him off in front of the hospital while I drove around looking for a parking spot. In the beginning it was easy but as the treatment continued, he became weaker and I always feared he would fall as he waited for me to come after I parked. He refused to go in until I was there with him. Lee was always protective of me and driving in Manhattan during the week was a challenge. But we made it through each day he had to be there. It was our only hope!

His youngest and only son from his second marriage was having his Bar Mitzvah in March so he postponed his treatment so he could fully celebrate the occasion. At the party he looked like he was living the life he always lived … happy, dancing and with no trace at all of what his body was going through. He did not have to pretend for that night, Lee could think of anything else but this happy occasion where he and I danced all night and the only time we slowed down was when we were dancing to a very sentimental song as we let our hearts speak to each other and listen to every love beat we had for one another. It was a night I wanted to keep going for I did not want to see morning again where reality begins to set in.

Soon after that memorable celebration, we were back to his appointments again. He had good days and some bad ones but he busied himself with work. I was glad to see that for I would be so sad seeing him just waiting for his life to pass him by. That was not Lee. I carried most of the fear for both of us because I felt it is the least I can do for him. Without him saying anything about his condition made me think he was putting up a face with me for I knew that Lee has certain emotional weights that he had carried for so long from his nasty divorce and adulterous behavior of his ex-wife. I also thought that she was a huge contributory factor in Lee's cancer because of the many stressful times she maliciously and intentionally hurt him by flaunting her amorous acts with her lover when he came to pick her up in the morning. Lee endured a lot and he did that for the sake of his son.

By April 1980 his condition did not improve but he was functional. I asked him to let me go home and get my kids who I had left in my parents care too long and who I needed to be with us as we struggled to win his battle with cancer. Arrangements were made with his two daughters and two of my friends to take care of Lee while I was away. It was bad enough I had to leave him at such bad timing but I had to do it. Lee's life was ending and I needed my children to be with me to start a new life without Lee. He also wanted them to be with him even if it was just for a short time.

Arrangements were made with my aunt in the Philippines and my children were good to go. The excitement of seeing my parents and siblings and cousins and the mere thought of having my kids on the same plane with me was met with very mixed emotions. One chamber of my heart was happy and the other chamber was very sad and worried. But it was a decision I had to make for the three people who lived in my heart. I only wanted to be away from Lee for the shortest time possible so within two weeks my children and I were in New York.

A little flashback: During the time that I had to leave my children with my parents, Lee had gone to the Philippines quite a few times and during those business trips, he would pick up Tyrone and Mia from work and take them with him to the hotel where they spent the week-end in the pool and sharing missing time from me. Lee always wrote or told me how well behaved my kids were and how he saw in Mia the simple things I did for him like fixing his coffee with enough milk and sugar. He adored my children and doted on them lavishly. He always teased me because out of the two luggages he took with him, only one was his as the other one was filled with goodies for everyone at home, most so for Ty and Mia. At that adjustment time, I substituted my presence in their lives with material things that I knew they would enjoy and be excited about. When Lee returned, I savored every details he told me about them and as I read their letters to me, I cried. I knew Lee knew how sad I was being away from them but we were just beginning a new life together and must prepare for their joining us.

There are certain events in our lives that happened which we sometimes prefer not to remember. Mine was on our way back to New York and we had a stop-over in San Francisco. My ex-husband and her sisters met us at the airport and took us out to dinner. That was the first time the father of my children saw him again after ten years of hiding from us and his responsibilities. I did it for the children so they may know him even for a brief reunion. Growing up they had no connection with him and there were no photos for them to remember him by. As expected, the kids showed no emotional connection nor warmth. They were in the presence of a stranger!

Back in New York, the new home for my son Tyrone and daughter Mia still so young to be fearful of a new environment but more so excited to find out what this America was all about, the land of the free, the country that would now changed our lives. As soon as we arrived home, Lee was full of life – for the first time after he was diagnosed, I saw him happy. I saw his blue eyes sparkled with delight as he lovingly looked at them. For a while we did not deal with his cancer. For a while we learned to have some life in the house. For a while, I had my handsome and adoring husband again. We made plans to go places with Ty, Mia and his son who had no problem adjusting to one another, and was more excited to have his new brother and sister in his young life. It was truly a wonderful reunion.

Arriving in April 1980, my kids missed two months of their schooling in the Philippines and it was too late to enroll in New York as in two months school was over. They had two months to be sad for leaving the only home they ever knew and the grandparents who loved them to death and the many cousins and friends they knew they will miss. But they also had the time to look forward to making new friends and attending a school that is quite different from what they had gotten used to in the Philippines. It was a different ball game but both were willing to play their parts. They made it easier on my heart to see that they were willing to adjust and not add any more stress that continues to build as my future with the man I loved became dim.

Lee wanted the children to see many places but we could not be gone too long as he tired too fast and I did not want to make his physical condition to be more obvious for fear it would only make him sad and even frustrated. His thinning hair was almost gone, his robust body was now void of stamina, his beautiful blue eyes still sparkled with love when he looked at me but there too I saw a sadness and words he did not want to utter. Lee put up a face for as long as he could but because we were of the same heart, I could read his mind and I could feel his heartbeats that were turned down a little bit.

Lee was a symbol of bravery as he battled the beast. The children were very attentive to him but without them knowing it, I would watch them as they walk away to the kitchen or their rooms. They had lots of unspoken words. I guess they felt if they did not ask, the beast would go away and as I watched them with Lee, I felt my family was finally complete for that moment and tomorrow will be a much better day. I carried lots of up and down emotions and I did faced this challenges with prayers and very strong faith in God. We hardly went to the synagogue unless there was an occasion or an event and more so then because of Lee's declining health. He always wore a Chai and I still look at his picture with it resting on his chest. I guess to him wearing it everyday meant he was closer to God!

The only drug we hoped would give him a 20% survival chance was not cooperating with his body and because of it he lost his appetite and hardly ate and for him that was really unheard of. Lee loved to eat ... we both loved to eat. He marveled on how I could eat with my bare hands especially when I am eating seafoods. But he marveled more at my peeling shrimps or separating crab meats for him but the ultimate peeling chilled grapes and dropping them in his mouth as we watched TV was probably the most unbelievable gesture that he loved with amazement!

By July 1980, it was apparent that another drug needed to be found and tried. By now Lee had lost more weight, his face was very sad and tired. Giving him a bath was a long process as it was not easy for him to stand under the shower for a long time so we tried the bathtub where he could at least sit down while I bathe him. We were okay with that. The problem was getting him to stand up and out of the tub. He would attempt several times to step out but he would lose his footing and I had to grab him before he fell. At that time I was probably 125 pounds so imagine me trying to hold on to him who weight about 180 pounds, dead weight!

I knew without him saying anything to me that he did not want to be a burden and all through this home care I gave him, never once did I think of him as a burden. I loved taking care of him and was always by his side. If I had to do some shopping I would ask a friend to stay with him and the children always wanted to be around should he needed something. They were very short shopping time for I really did not want to be away from him at all. What I feared happened one night. My nightmare!

I was not gone that long when my friend Evelyn Sinjian showed up at the grocery telling me to go back home immediately as Lee was seriously ill. I called the ambulance and he was taken to the hospital. There he remained for about two weeks so they could monitor his blood count.

Everyday became sadder for me each time I headed home after staying with him all day. It was the most difficult time for me to go home and not know what tomorrow would be but my children were too young to be left alone especially at night. It was then that I hired Elena Habaluyas, to be his private nurse. She was also from my country and Lee was very pleased with her and I later found out from Elena how he loved talking about me. I never knew then that fate would soon dictate a friendship that would begin after Lee was gone and was to last for many years.

Sadly, the chemotherapy was not cooperating again with Lee's body and he became weaker and almost resigned to his fate. We never talked how serious his cancer has gotten and I think it was only because we did not want to surrender to the beast and we did not even want to think our togetherness was in the brink of breaking. It was only when he finally was sent home that we touched the subject when he saw my tears coming down my face and asked me why I was crying. For the first time after he was diagnosed I let go all my inner feelings and sob so hard on his chest and as he stroke my head he kept saying "Please don't cry. Please don't cry" and all I could say was "I don't want you to leave me."

Having Lee home was a good thing for we were together most of the time as I sat by his bedside until he would fall asleep. For someone who did not have much of an activity, Lee was very tired. All he did was an effort and I knew then that he was not happy to see me be a nurse to him. It was quite ironic that he was surrounded with nurses when he was healthy and doing business in recruiting them and placing them in different States except California. And now that a real and experienced nurse is what we could avail ourselves with, it was now us, who have to pay but that is what life is all about – the wheels of life keep turning and we have no idea if we are up or down or simply going in circles as our lives have been patterned with.

For both our comfort, Lee slept in our bed while I slept in the next room but left his bedroom door open. We all adjusted to make him comfortable but not sleeping in the same room with him only made me half asleep as the other half of me was listening to him. I think subconsciously I was slowly detaching myself from him so when the time came, the pain of final separation would be easier to bear. So I thought!

A few days before Lee passed away, his lawyer friend, Herb Smith came with Lee's son-in-law Lowell Friedman and his mother Moira. I was in the room with Lee and Herb asked me if I could leave the room for a few minutes as they wanted to talk to Lee. Without thinking anything of it, I heeded the request. As fast as they came, so they left. When I went back to the room, Lee was still the same, just sitting upright and with very weak look in his eyes, he followed me as I sat down in the bed and I could tell he was very tired.

Three days after that very brief visit, Lee was sitting up and was barely awake. His mouth was slightly opened, saliva beginning to build up so I asked him to spit it out on the wastebasket that I line with lots of paper towel. When he attempted to spit it out, he could not and he just drooled over so I wiped his mouth with paper towel and his saliva was red!

I immediately called his older daughter Randi and she and Lowell came right away. As soon as Lowell saw him, he told me to throw away all the tissues and Q-tips I used to clean his mouth. He also told me not to touch anything as his gums were bleeding and it was not a good idea to keep him at home as the infections inside his body were now oozing out! I wanted to hug him so badly but I was cautioned not to touch him. For the first time in my life with Lee, and of all times in his life, I could not touch him. This could have been what I dreaded most and tried to be prepared with, but not this way. I wanted him in my arms, to hold him tight and not let him go. I wanted us to hold hands again like we always did. I wanted to be so near him so my energy could pass on to him and help him from being so weak. It felt like we were being separated by this monster in his body and his oozing blood was like a moat that I could not cross. I felt so helpless yet I remained strong and did not lose my composure.

Lee's eyes would open and close like he was drugged yet wanted to utter something but no words came out. I sat by his side as we waited for the ambulance to arrive. Sitting there and watching my wonderful husband slowly slipping away, my love for him took over me and I reached out for his hand and placed it between my two palms. I wanted our heartbeats to connect so I may infuse some life into him. I wanted Lee to just wake up and be the same man I saw walking out from the elevator wearing a big smile as he walked towards me. I wanted to see his hairy chest that peeked through his open shirt. I wanted to hear him laugh so loud and I wanted him to hold me tight and kiss me tenderly on my forehead. I wanted him to not go.

The day I feared most was drawing near and my heart begun the pain I did not want to feel. But how could I not feel pain when all my hopes and dreams for us all to be together was coming to an end? Was this pain selfishly meant for me alone or was I in pain for fear of losing the only man who came closest to the chamber of my heart? I knew the answer. No one can ever fill that void ~ that part of my heart that only belonged to Lee!

It was a long day and night and it was a very emotional one. It seemed like everyone was lost in their own thoughts. After receiving emergency attention, Lee was brought to his hospital room where we all gathered in almost deafening silence. He slept most of the time and I sensed there was no pain as he lay there so peacefully and perhaps unaware of my presence. Even after everyone had left, I stayed. I wanted him to see me when he came out of his deep sleep. I wanted him to know I had not left him. I wanted him to lift his hand to reach for mine. I wanted that so badly.

I pulled a chair next to his bed and I put my hand over his needled-arm. Maybe my heartbeat will let him know I was there. I could only wish that. I asked myself "Does he know how much I love him? Will he remember the happy times we spent together? The loving ways I peeled grapes for him as we sat in the living room watching TV? Will he remember the laughters we shared, the trips, the loving notes we wrote each other? Will he take these memories with him when he finally walked with his creator?" I knew then and I know now that I will always remember his love for me, It warms my body and my soul!

That night I stayed at the hospital. I called a friend of mine to stay with my children until I returned in the morning. My body was tired, my spirit was low. But my mind was on speed zone. Every once in a while I would glance at him with a "tinge of miraculous hope" that I would see those beautiful blue eyes again. I wanted to see his fingers move. I wanted to hear him call me "Angel". Nothing changed through the night and sleep was not my friend.

Before the nurse came in to clean him up, I decided to go home for a couple of hours and be back even before he knew I had left. I wanted to see my children and I needed a hot shower to wake up my tired body. I watched Tyrone and Mia walk to the bus stop, waved at them through the window pane, turned around and saw our bed. Lee was not there anymore and I felt so alone. The hospital bed was the only thing that cradled his tired body. I wished we had those days when we would spend hours and hours in bed, laughing and just feeling so secure. That feeling had passed me by and I had accepted that this was going to be a very long empty road I would be taking. As empty as it would be, knowing Lee was with me made it worth the journey. But how about Lee? Did he feel the same as I did? What was in his mind? Have I given him enough joy and memories to take with him? How would I be without him in my life? I prayed that when I got back at the hospital, he would be there sitting up!

I managed to nourish my body with whatever was in the frigs. In the kitchen across me, his chair stared at me and I was for a few seconds lost in a thought that had no meaning. Then the phone rang. I looked at the clock and it was eleven o'clock! It was the nurse calling and I held my breath in fear. She said "I am sorry Mrs. Kramer but your husband had passed away ". Just like that. "When?" I asked. "Just a few minutes ago. Please come to the hospital right now!" I did not scream but I cried silently and calmly, pulled myself together and prepared to leave. All I heard was me keep saying: "He did not wait for me, he did not even wait for me."

Even though I knew this moment was going to come sooner or later the reality of it all was something one cannot handle. I was in total shock! I hated myself for leaving the hospital, I thought I was being selfish in going back to the house to take care of me and the kids. What really drove me to do that? Was that a way of Lee sending me away so I would not see him take his last breath? Was he trying to spare me the sight of him losing his battle against cancer?

I told the nurse I would be there right away as I wanted to kiss him goodbye before they took him down. After making brief calls I drove back to the hospital and in the room was Lee, laying there peacefully. I bent over to kiss his forehead and I lost it. All the emotions I had stored inside me came out for I no longer had to pretend that I was hurting, that I was dying inside, that I was angry and that I was longing for him. My man who loved me from head to toe was gone. My love who inscribed in a bracelet the most precious message ever: "You are the Best thing that ever happened to me". I sat there, feeling numb or perhaps wanting to be numb so I could pinch myself and smile because it was only a bad dream. I was alone in that room, yet my world was so big I could only see Lee now so far away, so far he could not even see me reaching out to him. Wanting to hold his hands, to feel his heartbeat, his presence and to know he has not left me. My world was colored Black!

Following the Jewish tradition, arrangements were made by his children. All I remember was signing papers as my mind froze in time and the whole process was as dark as my emotions. I do recall Lowell coming over to the house to get his clothing and I picked the one he loved the most. They left me alone to mourn as I remember getting into the limo with his children while my son Tyrone and my daughter Mia rode with my friends. It just seemed, as I now try to recall and re-live that eventful day how numb inside I was, the reality had closed in on that chapter of my life with Lee. All the tears I had held back had taken the liberty to flow continously.

At the Temple while Lee lay in state, Lowell approached me quietly and sat next to me. As he leaned towards me he whispered "Is that how you want Lee to be dressed?" and I said "What do you mean?". He led me to the casket and lifted the cover. I looked in and almost burst into a loud laugh! There was Lee, with his favorite suit and tie and as I looked at his handsome face, there it was, his favorite sunglasses, neatly placed over his eyes! Lowell asked "Did you want him to wear those sunglasses?" and I said "Of course not. Take them off!". They must have been in his suit pocket and those who dressed him up thought they were part of his ensemble. Through tears of laughter I saw him laughing with me for even at the very end, Lee wanted to make me laugh, he wanted to see me happy! It was his way of saying goodbye to me …. in his most tender, natural and loving way!

I never realized until now that to be a widow at the age of 36 was as mysterious and frightening as going into a long tunnel and not knowing what lies ahead and how soon it would take me to see the light again. Lee was only 52 when he left us, too young to be cut off from a life he lived well with much passion and zest. But he also lived a very stressful 2nd marriage that ended in a divorce due to his wife's infidelity.. He lost so much including the custody of his only son which saddened him. During their divorce proceeding he was also mentally tortured by his wife's disrespectful nature.

Lee was buried at Mt. Ararat Cemetery in Farmingdale, New York. His first wife Honey and his mom Mildred Brown Kramer were buried there too. Deep down inside me I felt a tinge of resentment. It felt like I was giving him back to his late wife but this feeling came and went as quickly as it came to my thought. I consoled myself that he was back with his mother too. They were now together, and I know my mother-in-law is smiling and I need to move forward.

Going back to our place was as hard as saying goodbye to Lee. That night as I lay awake and crying, I remembered that very brief time we talked. He was sitting up on the bed and I sat at the edge next to him. It was time to talk and I begun to get teary-eyed and kept my head down low. With his tenderness, he lifted my face and asked what I was thinking of. I no longer wanted to hold back my pain and I said to him "I do not want you to leave me". With that he pulled me towards his chest and as he stroke my long hair that he loved, he said "Angel, I do not want to leave you too but this disease I have is beyond my control." For the first time since Lee was diagnosed, I cried hard and so did he.

While losing Lee was already embedded in my mind, I did not expect him to leave that soon even though the quality of his life was barely existing. Yet in my heart there was a sense of relief from the gnawing pain of his fast deterioration. I consoled myself of the thought of him gone with some dignity. For a man who looked to each day with lots of promises, I knew it was very difficult for him to see himself slowly change to a person he hardly knew.

A couple of weeks after Lee was laid to rest at Mount Ararat Cemetery, I was awakened by a sound of cracking glass. Fearful that someone was trying to get in through the sliding door, I turned all the lights in my bedroom, nervously peeked through the hallway and then turned all the lights. I waited... nothing. Walked to the kitchen, turned all the lights, then to the living room. Nothing. By now, the kids were up too and did their own checking of the apartment. Everything was fine. We all went back to bed with some of the lights left on! But I could not go back to sleep.

I lay there, wondering what was that all about. In the semi-darkness of the room, a sudden scent of perfume came through the room. It was so fragrant, a familiar scent. A calming aroma. Next thing I knew, it was already morning and it was time to get up. Towards the bathroom I went and was met by the same scent and this time it was much stronger. Just above the toilet was my little shelf where all the perfumes Lee gave me were displayed.

Still smelling the strength of the perfume, I stuck my nose close to each bottle and there it was, the brand new bottle of perfume Lee had last given me, the bottom was wet and when I lifted it, I heard a sound of broken glass and I saw that one side of the carton was slightly torn. I thought of Lee and the pleasure he derived just seeing me so delighted with more bottles of perfume.

Did Lee visit me that morning? Where I come from it has been said that when a loved one passes away without having said their last goodbye, their spirit lingers on for 40 days at which time they hang around with those they love. I do believe this to be true for it has happened before as told by those who had experienced it. Somehow, the thought that Lee was there that morning made me smile for I had always longed to feel his presence again. At least for that brief moment he made me feel loved one more time and when physical presence was a miracle, he sends signs that he and I alone understand. I miss him more so.

About a year after Lee's crossing over the bridge, my son Tyrone called me at our office to let me know that our apartment was burglarized! I told them to stay put and not touch anything and I rushed home. The front door lock was axed open and they ransacked every room. They took my expensive jewelries and even the monies that my son saved and hid in a box under his bed. How they knew where to look is beyond my comprehension. I felt so violated, disrespected and helpless even after the police came and did their routine investigation. It was a lost case and my heart was angry.

These low life people who entered our home were the thieves that yanked every memories we had and replaced it with fear and hate. They stole my necklace with a Chai and the beautiful solid gold bracelet that Lee lovingly doted me with. There were others and while they were material things, their value was beyond that. Something that money cannot buy nor replaced. These were Lee's act of thoughtfulness and sensitiveness towards our relationship. Lee was my "Knight in Shining Armor". He was my security, he was my love and he was my joy!

Was this suppose to help me heal? Were they the ones who were destined to take away the special material proofs of Lee's sweetness and thoughtfulness so I may be left with memories in my heart? I wish I knew the answer ~ maybe it would somehow ease the yearning pain in my insides. Yet knowing how much he loved me, was enough to put a bandage on my open wound.

With all the innocence within me and all the trust I gave those around me, I never in my wildest imagination foreseen what was going to happen next! At the reading of Lee's Will which was produced by his lawyer friend Herb Smith three or four days before he passed away and without my presence, as Herb Smith asked me to leave the room for a few minutes. His intention was to make Lee sign his Last Will with Lowell Friedman and his mother Moira Friedman as witnesses. I was young, I was void of the "smarts" in subjects such as this. Who would even think that they would do this to Lee. Right there on his deathbed, they tricked him into signing the Will which obviously was made to benefit the children and basically made me an outsider.

At the home of Randi and Lowell Friedman, the Will was read and I felt so alone, like I was in a lion's den and they were ready for a kill. They took advantage of my trust in Lee and in them. They connived and schemed together without even thinking how disrespectful that was to Lee!

Everything I heard, every word that was spoken were like daggers in my heart. The room was so cold with people filled with greed. They offered to give me $10, 000.00 in exchange to giving up my position as Vice President at RANK International, Lee's new company that symbolized his freedom from his ex-wife. In the Will, it read that I was suppose to receive 30% of the business and the rest were divided among the three children. The shock came after.

Much earlier in our marriage, Lee told me that because he was still going through divorce when he opened RANK International, he was advised by Herb Smith that it was best to put the business under the name of his oldest child so that his ex-wife cannot go after the company should she win the divorce. I understood that and was assured by him that once the divorce was over he would change the ownership to solely under his name. I trusted and I did not ask again.

So now I was told that while Lee left me 30% of the company, I was not going to get anything because the company was not under his name but under Randi's. I never thought to ask them to show me the documents and I believe that even if I did ask, lots of scheming had been done and Lee was no longer capable of being bothered with all these documentations. Besides he too trusted Herb Smith.

That evening came and went and I was filled with renewed anger, pain and felt so violated by the same people I thought were family to me and a loyal friend of my husband. My world crumbled one more time. I refused the $10,000.00 and crying heavily, I walked away from the meeting. I did not want to have anything to do with all of them. They betrayed me and they betrayed Lee! My heart was so broken but my spirit was soaring with pride for in my mind, I did not want these kind of people in my life. Money is the fruit of all evil and they were all devils in my eyes! They were all Jewish and did not believe in Jesus Christ, but surely, Judas lived in their being. Judas was a symbol of Betrayal!!!

One winter night, the doorbell rang and I looked out from my second floor window and saw Lowell and Mike. I went to the door and very coldly, they said "we are here to take your car" the very same car my mother-in-law Mildred bought me as her appreciation for my caring ways with her. I went back upstairs and hysterically called my father-in-law Stanley in Tennessee. I told him what was happening and what he said to me sounded like thunder and came with a lightning that penetrated my heart one more time. He said "give them the car because you are no longer family!" If my mother-in-law was still around, this would not have happened. The only two people who loved me were gone. I was on my own and had to swim harder against the current for once again, I was betrayed, this time by Lee's father! I should have known he was a mean person because my mother-in-law was so unhappy living with him for he only thought of Stanley when all she wanted was to see Lee more than once a year!

Like an obedient child and with anger and hatred in my heart I handed them the key to the car. Did I do the right thing then? Was I suppose to fight for my right? But the car was registered under the company name and pride took over me that night. As far as my feelings were concerned, they too were no longer family to me! I planted a seed of resentment towards them all …. even towards Lee. I felt he did not protect me from this money-hungry family. How could he have left me without assurance and security? Why did he not change the company name back to him? Or did he? That day Herb

Smith came with Lowell and his mother and asked me to leave the room, could Herb changed the company document back to Randi? The more I thought about it, the more I blamed myself for not being smart enough not to have stayed in the room. I was his wife and I should have been there. Trust had changed its meaning since then. I had lost control of my life with Lee. For a moment, I felt I no longer belonged in his life but then again, was this surprise visit suppose to alter all that I believed in and all that Lee and I had together?

I learned later on from Stanley's live-in housekeeper Flora that our former office secretary Linda Campo and Sylvia St. John my friend for over 15 years, have been calling Stanley telling him what I was doing with my life and have told him I had been dating! They said lies and gossiped about me. Flora, during their New York visit took me on the side and warned me about Linda and Sylvia and that I should not trust both of them. I completely severed contact and Flora was right. I sat in the living room with my kids who were wondering why my car was taken away. They too felt the sadness that surfaced in me and the disbelief of how cruel some people can be!

**"Grief never ends**.... but it changes. It is
a passage, not a place to stay.
Grief is not a sign of weakness, nor a lack of faith.
It is the price of love! "
(Marcia Genoveva Bundalian)
January 5, 2016

I found a job in Manhattan with Blue Cross Blue Shields as a Claims Examiner. I worked to supplement my resources and it also broadened my mind about life in the United States outside the comfort of our own business. With my detaching from Lee's immediate family and friends, I was able to cope inspite of the challenges of a new beginning. To add insult to an injury, my landlord decided to raise my rent. Was this another cruel doings of Lee's family? The way they were, anything was possible for I now see them as a source of meanness, sadness, betrayal and greed!

Without Lee, I knew and was prepared to budget especially because I was cut off from Lee's business and family. The only support I got was from my wonderful son Tyrone and daughter Mia who both worked at the groceries after school. Whatever they earned was theirs and while I still took care of most of their needs, they were both very independent and helped me in more ways I could ask for.

So we moved from Bayside to a two story duplex in Flushing and we lucked out because we got the top floor. I heard it said before that we must continue going higher and higher, including our place of residence. When Lee and I started our life together, we lived in the first floor of a three story apartment complex, which was cozy for the two of us. We had an entrance to the side of the building which made it easy when we came home. Two and half years later, the second floor got vacated and we moved in. So I was moving on up and was not about to settle for a new place below the second floor.

Now a new chapter of our lives was about to begin in Flushing. When the top floor became reasonable enough to rent, we grabbed it and lived there for almost six years. Our lives begun to change after that as my son Tyrone was not happy living in New York and moved in with his father in Southern California. I figured that perhaps a male influence in his life was needed and though sad I was inside, I agreed and sent him on his way. I did not realize until much later on how independent and strong he was. He was ready to tackle another change in his journey, to live with almost a total stranger who has not learned to be a father nor act like one.

One night, Tyrone called me, very upset and desperate to leave his father's residence. They had a bad fight and when a child has an anger towards a parent who abandoned him when he was a toddler, the anger that has settled in his mind and heart eventually would come out when provoked or when it is the right moment. I called my sister Ludette who was at that time married to Larry Crisler and asked her to please go and pick up Tyrone and have him stay with them for a while until Mia and I arrived. They were so generous and kind and understanding and even enrolled Tyrone at Nogales High School where he finished and graduated. My sister and Larry were my saving grace! Their hospitality and taking full responsibility of my son is one gesture in my life that I will be forever grateful for.

This turn-around incident brought back memories of the past, of the man I married who was not emotionally and financially ready to be a husband and more so to be a father. This thought alone was not worth keeping in my mind for it was a dead issue just like he was to me and my children. This thought I erased and focused on how lucky I was for having my son safe and loved in my sister's home.

Accepting and recognizing the need to change and live for the present, I begun to accept social invitations from my few chosen male friends. One of them held me up in a pedestal, treated me like I was fine china, a delicate work of art! He adored me from head to toe and would not even let me carry a bag of groceries. He chose the color of my clothes, where I went, who I went with. He called me at least three to four times a day, saw me every single day, seven days a week!

In the beginning it seemed wonderful and I felt very loved and protected and quite flattered. As our relationship became more intense, I begun to sense that I was slowly being controlled and my friends started to thin out. We did not have a lover's quarrel. We had fights. One week-end, I decided to go dancing with my two girlfriends. When I called my kids to check on them they told me how many times he had called. It basically ruined my fun evening and when I got back home, he was there! He was fuming with madness and we ended up fighting and while we had fought many times before, over his jealousness and possessiveness, I never really put much into it. This time I got the message loud and clear,

I learned to clam up. I decided I would do what I wanted to do. This attitude brought more fights and arguments and my heart started to turn cold. No matter how often we made up, the reality of it all, being imprisoned and being controlled within my own freedom became the strongest decision I made to move to California. This move would also bring back our small family together.

I knew that if I did not move away from New York the now bad relationship would escalate and my feelings for him would definitely continue to go downhill. I was ready to move on and after six years of not evaluating the relationship to the fullest, it was time I did. There was no more room left.

So on August 12, 1986 my daughter Mia and I boarded the plane for California. I will not deny that I cried a lot – because of the good memories I was leaving behind, not just my life with Lee but my pristine relationship with the man who loved me so deep that it suffocated me. I am finally free – and in a few hours I would set foot on another place where I intended to let my head and not my heart rule my life! Cruising above the clouds, I felt the lightness of my entire being. I saw a rainbow without rain and sun. For a brief moment, I questioned myself whether it was really there or was I just imagining it.

That was the sign I was looking for.... I knew then that what happens to me depended on how I see things around me and how I perceive them to be. For the first time in six years I was ready to face another chapter of my life with the greatest expectations and with the highest form of self-preservation. I knew there will be challenges along the way but I also knew that I had become wiser, less gullible and that life will continue to be like the rainbow ... beautiful after each rain, unreachable and untouchable but yet it promises a pot of gold at each end! It is always good to believe that beyond each ray of colors is the beauty of our lives as we live it!

I did not have a lot of money so we brought basically what we needed to get settled. I had my car and belongings shipped so we had to find a place of our own. We were so fortunate because I saw this AD in the papers of a townhouse in West Covina very close to where my sister lives and the school where Tyrone went was a walking distance away. Because of these good tidings that I've showered me with, I could not be any humbler but rather grateful to God for watching over us!

So here I was in Southern California. Everything about New York was wrapped carefully and tenderly inside my heart. My new horizon was just beginning to show and I had to move on and think stronger and act wiser. I will not deny that there were moments when my mind would go back to New York and allow my past life to re-run in my head. I wanted to feel the happiest and the saddest moments of my life there and always picked the strongest moment which made me grateful for the life I had with Lee even though it was short-lived.

My daughter Mia and I arrived in Southern California on August 12, 1986 and by October 1986 I had a job with Acorn Engineering at the City of Industry where I worked for nine and a half years. I went through job hunting, far and near but it seemed that Acorn Engineering was meant for me. I saw the AD in the morning papers, drove to the company, met with the HR Manager who later called on Pat Lyman to interview me. There was no need for a second interview. I was hired right there! What a beautiful way to start my renewed life and I knew then that my children and I would be alright.

I worked as Customer Service Representative, covering 24 States together with my thoughtful and wonderful Manager Bob Clinkenbeard. Our work ethics were great and outside of the office we were friends. Unfortunately, Bob had already lost one lung to cancer as he was a heavy smoker during his younger years. His office was next to the kitchen door and my cubicle was across his office. During that time smoking was allowed and tolerated but the issue was everyone smoked in the kitchen and the door was left wide open so he and I were directly in the path of the second hand smoke. This is when I noticed his breathing was labored and was affecting him. One afternoon, I decided I best talk with Dart who was the secretary of owner and President, Carl Morris. I shared with Dart my concern in having the kitchen door wide open and us being subjected to the second-hand smoke and of course used Bob as a first hand reason to keep the doors closed at all times.

About a week after my conversation with Dart, there at the door was a sign posted "Keep This Door Closed"! It felt so good to see that Management had listened to my plea and for that I was very grateful to Dart as she was my voice with Mr. Morris. Bob too was grateful.

It was 1987 when my son Tyrone brought in the mail and sat down with me and handed me an envelope and said "Ma, check this out?" and I did. It was from Southern California Connection, a Club that was also known as the "Millionaire's Club". He encouraged me to become a member and start socializing again. So I took his admonition and went to the club where I was given all the usual sales pitch that was so common in places like that.

What I liked about it was I was the one to decide whether I would like to meet someone who had picked me and I was the one who would pick the person of interest. The guidelines were simple. We had a library where our profiles were filed and a video room as well. The office would send out notices of anyone who would like to meet us and all we did was go to the office, take out the file and video of that particular gentleman and make a decision. I did not personally pick anyone. I felt that I should be the one who would go through the process of elimination and there were quite a few who I chose to meet which were only first dates and that was it. I was not in a rush so that worked well with me.

I met one who was in the military and was in combat. His name was Paul. He was a very tall guy and was not the fine-looking man I preferred but he was very nice and thoughtful. We went out a few times, nothing serious as it bothered me when he would turn on the TV and watched Hamburger Hill over and over and would go in a position like he was in the battlefield. He actually scared me so I would excuse myself and leave and he was fine with that. There was just a friendship we were trying to build and perhaps a companionship for two people whose past lives had left us with sad memories.

I saw less of Paul because there was no point but we did stay connected and every now and then we would go dancing which I love to do. One time, while sitting out the music, I noticed these four women sitting at a table close to us who were having too much fun. One of them came over and asked me if they could borrow Paul and I of course said "Yes" and Paul loved it so off they all went to the dance floor and went crazy dancing. I sat there and watched him make a fool of himself and when the music stopped, he stood there by himself and with his index finger, motioned me to go and join him. I did not get up until he came over and extended his hand to dance with me. By then I realized he had too much to drink and I was not going to be a part of it. While we were doing a fast dance, he tried to lean back and as he did that he started to fall while he was holding my right hand. He was a big guy and it was very easy for him to bring me down so I remove his hand from mine and let him fall to the floor!

I walked back to the table, took my belongings and waited for him to return and then I told him we were leaving. I drove him home, took his car and I went home. I still cannot recall how he got his car back but he did. That was when I decided no more Paul. But he still would call and invite me but the answer was always a "no". I do remember what time he took me home and my kids were waiting outside and he made a comment to them "I will take care of your mom" and that he did when I needed a friend.

My Nissan Sentra was a used car when I bought it in New York. It had reached its lifespan and I was without a car and needed one so badly to get me to work. So I called him and without hesitation, he and his friend brought his extra car to me which I used for quite some time. He was just as happy as having his car to connect with me and remain good friends. He knew I did not have the money to buy even a used car. I needed time to save up for even a down-payment and his generosity came at such needed time!

I came home one day from work and there was this envelope from the Southern California Connection. I was chosen by Anthony P. Stephen. All I needed to do was go and check him out. So I did and my life begun to take off on another journey. I went to the Library and pulled out his file and settled myself in one of the private cubicles. One of the first thing I came across was his religion. He was a catholic like me. My first marriage was to a Protestant who only converted to Catholic so we could be married in the church. He did not really practice nor was he a church-going Protestant. Then I married my Knight in Shining Armor Lee Perry Kramer who was Jewish who practiced his religion not as religiously as he would have wanted to but he always observed the High Holidays.

I thought to myself that perhaps I should marry my own kind. Maybe my marriage would last and longer. But it was too soon to go in that direction so I responded to Tony's invite and a few days later after submitting my response, he called me. We made a date to meet for coffee. He lived in Chino and I lived in West Covina, a mere twenty five minutes drive. He got lost and called me as it was getting late and asked me if we could just have dinner. He finally found his way to my condo and we went to dinner. Conversation was good, lots of laughter and sharing of thoughts. He also lost his spouse to cancer so we had a common story to share. The evening ended nice and he asked to see me that week-end. We did a lot of day activities which were mostly driving to nearby towns. Evening dates were limited to dinner or movies as he was not a dancer like Lee. But he had a very secured job with Honeywell and later on with Hughes Aircraft when Honeywell moved to another State and he did not want to relocate. By the way, I never called him Anthony. To me he was "Tony"!

One of his good qualities that I liked was he went to church on Sunday so most of the time we did not see each other on Sundays but that was good to a certain point. Tony was very generous and would surprise me with small gifts. One time we were in Solvang and in the store where there were lots of knick-knacks, while I was browsing I heard something fall and the store manager walked towards Tony and I heard them talking. He was apologizing profusely as one of the figurine had dropped and its pony tail broke. He insisted on paying for it and with his dimpled smile he handed it to me. It was a Precious Moment little girl in ponytail! That made me see another side of him that made me think. He was a very responsible man with an honorable character. That day in Solvang, he got an extra point for that simple gesture of doing what was right.

We continued to see each other and he always made sure that when he took me home, there was already another date for the following week-end. I realized then that he was getting seriously affected and did not want to give other interested party the opportunity to spend time with me. As I had previously shared, Paul was a kindhearted guy who really had a soft heart that was not hardened by his life in the battleground. He never called me to ask back his car. He really did not need it so I was so blessed by his sweet gesture. During one of his visits, Tony asked me why I was driving such a big car with six cylinders and I simply said "because I do not have a car and my friend Paul let me use it for as long as I needed it". I guess that did not sit well with him because with the car in my possession came the opportunity for Paul to continue being in touch with me. I did not make anything out of it.

But deep in his mind, Tony was being bothered by it. So one night as we dined at a nice restaurant, he said to me: "I have been thinking about the car you are using and I think it is too big for you. How about us going to the car dealer this week-end and we will get you a car?" I said that it would be wonderful but I had no money to buy a car and he said "don't worry about that "!

So there he proved his intentions to me. He put down a thousand dollar and I got my Toyota Tercel. I just cannot recall if he paid for the rest or not nor was it a used car? I believe I was beyond belief that I got a car that fast and without conditions …. Oh yes ….

There was a condition and that was for me to return Paul's car which I did immediately which also ended my contact with him. So Tony and I continued to see each other and one afternoon he took me to his house in Chino. He had an acre property, no plants, no walkway and the house was little to be desired. The patio was dirty from dirt that was mostly made by the gophers. The inside of the house was dark and the furniture were old with heavy dirty drapes. His two sons Eddie and Dennis, then high schoolers were at the living room when we walked in. Nothing was said much between us as we immediately went to the back. I saw the potentials that would be possible but kept that thought in my head,

April 1988 my father who was living in the Philippines was found on the bedroom floor unconscious and was taken to the hospital where he layed in a comatose condition. As soon as I got the call, I immediately called Tony and booked my flight. My sister Ludette who had visited him two years ago decided not to go as she wanted to remember our dad the way he was the last time she saw him. I understood that and while my brother Joey said I should not go home because my dad was gone, I was bent on going home to say my goodbye to my dad, the man I had put in a pedestal, the father who loved me like no other did. He was my pen pal and was my inspiration. He was my mentor. He was my protector! He was my dad who I loved with the deepest feeling a daughter could have. The legal size, lined yellow pad will no longer be needed and the crossword puzzles unsolved!

I had a window seat and there was only one passenger on the aisle seat. I was lost in sorrow as I cried quietly. I heard him say "are you okay?" I turned to him and mumbled "Not really. My father just passed away and I am going home". His reply was that of a gentleman and he continued conversing with me perhaps to take my mind off my sadness. He told me he has an ivory business in Africa while he picked up his briefcase. He said he had two ivory pendant and would appreciate it if I would help him decide which one appeals more than the other. He took them out and laid them on the briefcase. One was circular in shape and the other was like a lion with detailed mane. He asked me which one I liked and I pointed at the lion. He thanked me and proceeded to close his briefcase, set it down and thanked me again with a smile that was sincere. I smiled back and said "welcome". Then he opened his hand and the Lion pendant was there. He said "This is for you. I want you to have this because you like it." I refused it but he kept on insisting in a nice way and so I accepted it. He gave me his business card and said he hopes we would be on the same flight going back. I said "that would be nice" as he was a good conversationalist and quite thoughtful with his gesture. But we did not see each other and I never thought of the business card he gave me. Looking back now I realized that I was being consoled by a total stranger in my moment of distress! I still have the pendant!

From the airport I was met by my older sister Vilma Damasca and we went straight to the funeral parlor. After paying my respect to my mother and other family clan, I walked up to where my father was lying in state. Looking dignified like always. His facial features were so prominent and he was a very handsome man, My Dad! I cried and sob quietly out of my respect for him. Silently and almost in a whisper I said "You did not wait for me Daddy. I wanted to hold your hand so you would know I was home. I am so sorry for not writing you for a long time. Forgive me for all the heartaches I caused."

It was my father who held us all together. My mother's silent strength was the knot that tied us. They were not the typical parents that made plans for their children. They guided us, provided for all our needs and yes, spoiled us in a very good way. No one was spoiled rotten even our youngest sister Ludette who was obviously favored by our mother. Yes, she did take advantage of that for a while but that ended at about the age of five when my mother finally saw she made trouble for all of us. Sadly, that sudden end of her spoilage became a reason for her meanness towards our sister Fatee. They were always on each other's case but this time my mother did not take any side. So they both grew up and learned to be sisters!

When I went home that night from the funeral parlor, I went to my dad's bedroom and sat on his bed and cried uncontrollably. I had spent so many hours in that bedroom, listening to his lectures on life and watching from the small TV his favorite show "Mission Impossible" and there on one wall was his collections of paperback novels of Earl Stanley Gardner. He was a crossword puzzle addict and his day did not start until he had his very strong black coffee and the newspaper he read from page to page saving the crossword page as his ultimate prize for the day. This I believe made his brain very healthy and his memory so great. Thank God, he never showed signs of forgetfulness!!!

The night before his burial, I went to his room and took one of his lined yellow legal size sheet and propped myself on the bed There I penned my last letter to my Dad. I let out every feelings I held in my heart. I apologized for not writing to him, told him how much I loved him and thanked him for that special love he doted me with.

At the gravesite before they closed his coffin, we all walked by to say our last goodbye. With my letter in my hand, I stepped closer and said my goodbyes and gently placed my letter by his side.

There was not enough tears to shed that moment. My heart was broken into pieces only to be mended with the thought that he went away with my letter and he will always have me as his pen pal. It was the bridge of love between my father and Candy, his pet name for me!

With the sudden demise of my father and having to go back home for his funeral, my contact with Tony was cut short. I had no time to think of anyone else but my children and my father. It was a very sad trip to the Philippines and worst was leaving my mother behind under the care of my brother Joey and sister Vilma. Who would have thought that both would only bring heartaches to my mom? There is no such thing as regret from the start. There is no such thing as hind sight from the start. And no matter what life throws at us, we either catch it, miss it or even are oblivious to it. So I have learned to grab as much as I can and then shift through them and let those that will not be positive for me just drop down or fall over. We are suppose to be learning as we go along and discard those that only bring us down. It is not easy to do that but once I went in that direction, my life and associations have been so much better.

When I returned, my relationship with Tony became more solid and I did not spend anymore time with Paul nor did I entertain other suitors. It was December 31, 1988 when Tony and I spent a beautiful week-end in Claremont where we went to a Christmas dinner show, then to the New Year's Eve party. There at the stroke of midnight, while at the dance floor, Tony proposed to me and with a smile, I accepted! A few days after that, we went shopping for my engagement and wedding ring, and his wedding ring.

I sat down with my son Tyrone and we talked about my engagement and ultimately, the wedding. Because he was living with me I wanted to know what his plans were so I would know how to fix the House so he could come with me. There was another room we could turn into his bedroom but he must have been toying with the idea of not coming with me. At that time, my daughter who was married to Tony P. was living in a two bedroom apartment. Tyrone told me he had discussed it with Mia that he and his then girlfriend Rachel would move in with them.

This is what my son Tyrone is all about. For such a young age, he was very matured in his ways and thinking. Much as I would preferred he stayed with us, I knew he had enough reasons to be on his own and save me any issues that may come out with living with a stepfather and his two sons. Looking back now, I am grateful for his wisdom and for his sensitiveness to an environment that could trigger any uncomfortable situations. This also showed me that I brought him up well and this was going to be a test to what he had learned living without a father figure but with quite a dominant mother.

The wedding was very nice. It was held at the Hyatt in West Covina on their outdoor veranda wedding area where the sky was just above us and the stars gave a special effect on that magical night where we vowed to be wed in sickness and in health, for poorer or richer and all that sounded good to start our life together. It was close-knit in that it was family and only close friends, about 55 of us. There was this small elevated area where a gazebo stood and underneath the brightness of the moon, stood my son Tyrone who gave me away, Tony's two sons, Eddie and Dennis and on the other side stood my daughter Mia, my niece Tisa and Rachel, soon to be Tyrone's wife. The reception was right there so it was hassle-free and everyone had a great time especially dancing the night away.

Two friends of mine flew all the way from New York, Elena Habaluyas and Nilda. Their presence did make me feel how truly close we were yet deep inside there was a spot missing. Our other dear friend Evelyn Sinjian-Forman who a couple of years earlier was on the Korean Airline Flight 007 that was shot down by the Soviets for reasons that the plane was in their territory and became a threat. Someday, I shall write about this for Evelyn was a dearest friend whose presence in my life during my sad days in New York made it a little easier to take. Someday her story will be told.

For our honeymoon we went to Hawaii ~ not my choice as I wanted to go to Europe but Tony said we would do that another time. Hawaii to many is paradise but to me the Philippines offered the same perhaps even more but that was our first trip together so we made the most of it. It was nice and we had fond memories of it mostly when we went snorkeling where my fear of deep sea water became a reason for panic. Tony was more into it, diving and snorkeling deeper while I hang on to dear life on a raft that had a magnified hole big enough for my face to fit in!

The day we arrived in Hawaii, I basked in the afternoon sun. The next morning my thighs were burned and my lips were swollen and I looked liked I had botox injection done! Yes, that was not a very good way to start my honeymoon but it was another reason for us to have a laughing session. That too was the last time I basked in the sun and the only time I was out on the beach was when the sun had come down and the only thing there for me to enjoy was the beauty of the setting sun. It was a wonderful week and there was much to look forward to once we were back home. So I thought.

There was never a time that we were by ourselves because his two sons lived with us and while their rooms were at the other side of the house, we still had the kitchen and living room as a common area. They did have their own bathroom which I tried to keep neat and clean but somehow, one of them was bent on making my life there unpleasant. They knew I did not want clothes and towels on the floor yet one of them always managed to leave them no matter how many times I would hang the towel on the rack. This issue became a sore on my side and sharing it with Tony went to deaf ears or perhaps went to the deaf ears of his boys.

His boys never did anything in the house. They acted like we were to serve them and if their dad asked them to mow the lawn, he would have to pay them. Then they have this attitude of making a list of things they want to eat and need and my husband would get whatever was on the list. They were old enough to get part time jobs but there was not a bone in their body that desired that. They were there to make sure their father provided for them. High school came and went and now they were suppose to be in college. The older one Eddie did enroll and was pretty serious with his studies. The younger one Dennis was just doing what his father told them in agreement: that for as long as they were in school they could stay with us! So Dennis took one or two subjects each year none of which was connected to a career but pipe dreams. This too became a sore on my side which Tony just shrugged off each time I would bring it up.

By this time, there was an obvious distance between us three and Tony never made any effort to help ease the air and animosity building within us. His role was a breadwinner, he had dinner and life went on. Thank God I was working because if I was not, something would finally have ended our marriage. But something really did happen and I cannot recall the onset of it but Eddie and I had an altercation in the den and while we were at it, Tony just sat there watching TV. It came to a point where Eddie called me a Bitch and pushed me so hard that the curtain hanging by the door came down with the rod and I ending up where the washer and dryer were! I went to the kitchen and took out a knife and rushed back to the den where Eddie was still standing, almost waiting for me to return. With the knife in my hand I pointed it at him and said "do that to me again and I will kill you!". Tony finally got up from his sunken sit area and told Eddie to leave and took the knife from my hand. That was it. No apologies. No calming me down. No sympathy. No freaking concern. That was the beginning of my clamming up, of losing my respect for him as my husband. I felt then that I was all alone to fight this battle and that I could not depend on him for emotional support. I became an army of my own war.

Work was an escape for me. Through my work Tony and I did something together as I joined the bowling team and invited him to join as well. But everyday, come 5:00 p.m. I dreaded going home. I even appreciated the traffic on the 60 freeway as this slowed me down from getting home. The mere sight of Eddie's truck on the driveway, made my blood boil. While there were four of us in that house, I was only talking to one … Tony! By then the two found ways to be out of the house as much as they possibly could. Fights were over …. Just silent animosity.

One morning, around 10:00 Tony came to our room, rubbing his hands in excitement. No not that kind of excitement as he told me quietly that Eddie was leaving. I almost screamed "WHAT?" He said he got a call from the place he found by the beach and that morning, he was moving out before someone else made an offer. I never saw Tony so elated as he jumped up and down with that big smile of his that showed his dimples! Sad thing was Eddie and I never made up and I really liked him but the situation in the house contributed to a not very healthy living conditions among the four of us. No goodbyes were said. I just watched him load up and then leave by peeking through the drapes. It was a good news yet it saddened me the way we parted. One out, one more to go!

As soon as his car was out of sight, I went to his room. It smelled smoky though I never saw him smoke. Then a general clean-up was done and after a day or two his room was my office. Having two windows that I could open and air out was perfect and it provided so much lighting that it made me feel alive. Here was a place of my own, no one to share it with. But across my office was Dennis's room which did not bother me. He pretty much kept to himself or sat in the den with his dad watching TV. I had a feeling that after Eddie left, he had finally thought of what he would do with his life. He also would have wanted to be out of that house as fast as he could and I understood.

For some very strange reasons, I cannot recall the episode of Dennis finally flying out of the nest. All I remember was he found a job with UPS in Ontario and I had told him how proud I was of him and I meant that too. He stayed with us for about two years until he found another job as a Forest Ranger in Chino Hills where he had a house to live in for a minimal rent. I never saw the house but was assured he was safe there. Even though we had a rough beginning, I was still concerned for him. Tony told me he did not think Dennis would amount to anything, unlike Eddie who finished college and had a very good job and was very sociable.

And here is Dennis, showing us the least of our expectations and he was finding jobs that were solid and with good benefits. He looked for every opportunities and kept moving on as a Forest

Ranger all the way up North. Everyone was free. We all moved on and settled down finally!

There were many things I changed in that house. Threw away the old furniture, took down the heavy and dusty drapes and finally brought some light into the living room. There was a bar between the kitchen and the living room which I hated because not only did it make the area look smaller, I did not care for it. I told Tony I wanted it taken out and he said No! I told him if he did not do it I would take an axe and start breaking it down and I told him I meant it. Seeing the seriousness in my face and tone of voice, he found someone to do it and I was happy! That got the ball rolling in the many changes I did in that house. We had a portable dishwasher which I hated because I have to manually attach the nozzle to the faucet and if it is not done right or tight enough, be ready to get squirt! So I asked him if we could put a built-in one and Tony's reply was: "it cannot be done as there isn't enough room for it under the counter plus we would lose storage space". With such a response I asked him "Are you a plumber? How in heaven's name would you know if it would fit or not? So off we went to Home Depot and got my new built-in dish washer!

The area where the old portable dish washer stood was now empty. So an idea came to mind as I looked at the stove and frigs, side by side. I asked Tony to please come to the kitchen as I had a question for him. He did come willingly and perhaps silently asking himself what now? My question was simple: "Does the frigs have to be there next to the stove?" and his answer was a No and a Why. I calmly answered him with a question: "Do you think the frigs would look better there where the dishwasher used to be so it would not be too crowded by the stove?" His reply was what I had hoped for. The windmills in my mind were spinning! I remember a saying that I applied: "Strike while the iron is hot!"

Well, that did not apply to Tony who became cautious whenever I want to change something. He always said "every time you open your mouth it is causing me money!". Did that offend me? You bet it did and it got deposited in one chamber of my heart. Later on, more hurting words piled in and soon my world changed!

We changed, both of us but we managed to stay together. We were not different from our friends and neighbors who had problems of their own. But marriage to me at this point had to be the last! I did not want to divorce but each day became more hurtful than the others. Pretty soon I just clammed up and lived each day like it was okay. What else was there for me to do? Tony had some good side that I appreciated but we were not one. We became roommates but cared about each other especially when we have doctor's appointments. Moving to the other side of the house was ideal.

Life was quiet. Any social events we went together were mostly family-related. We were both so busy with our jobs that coming home and dining together became non-existence! He ate at the den and I ate in the kitchen. What really bothered me then was after making dinner, I would dish out his meal and he walks to the den not even waiting for me to be done with mine! That was the beginning of our separate lives!

It was April 5, 2005 when he came after watching baseball with his son Dennis. He was frantic as he could not find his car keys. Came home to get his spare and I drove him to the Chino Hills parking lot. In the car we started conversing and I was asking him questions which annoyed him. Just before we got to the parking lot, he said to me "Marcia, this is why I do not want to ride with you. You ask too many questions". So I said: "When you have friends riding with you, are they okay to talk and ask questions?" That started the defensiveness and more argument. Then he said: "Why don't you accept that we just Co-Exist?"

I stopped the car and said: "Remember this day Tony. You are the one who closed the door on our marriage. You also have refused to go to counseling. You have closed your door on me much much earlier and I stayed because I wanted this marriage to work. Now you have ended it." His reply was "okay" and he got out of the car, walked to his car and drove off!

The way the house was set up was perfect for our situation. He was at the East side and I was on the West side with the kitchen and living room as a common area although he always stayed in the Den. He also told me that he would take care of his meals and I should just buy what I needed. What an Arrangement I thought! We stopped arguing and annoying one another but we did have small talks that concerned the house and our jobs. Separation became a solution and we managed to be very cordial and respectful to each other. We even became perfect roommates!

We talked about what would be the best thing with regards to the house and we both agreed that It was not a good time to sell. Real Estate was way down low so he told me that we should just go about our business and for me to go wherever I please and can stay in the house anytime I want. We did have quite a number of arguments which stemmed mostly about money as I was not working anymore and because of his advice to me when I was let go by the Engineering Company I worked for about 9-1/2 years, Tony suggested I just continue my little home based business with Jafra Cosmetics! So I took his advice but did not focus on my business in the true sense of the word. I did not have that Ambition to move up higher than a Manager and with that I lost the opportunity to really make a good Business out of Jafra. There was no doubt I enjoyed it but I was more after making other women feel good about themselves than me making buco-bucks! The Director position did not appeal to me for I saw myself so far from being a business woman! Others saw it but my vision was elsewhere! I was content. I felt peaceful yet there was a certain void in my life. No, I did not pine for Tony's love and devotion. I knew it was there. There was just this feeling of being with someone yet there is no one there to hold hands with, and snuggle while watching TV. I felt alone many times but I turned that into something more like having the space I needed. Soon the same space got bigger and in the center I stood ... unreachable!

I decided I was not going to begrudge Tony for the outcome of our marriage for I had taken the fair share of some responsibility of our broken marriage. They say it takes two to tango, so there it is!!!

We both ventured out and did our own thing but we never asked each other about what we were doing, Who we were seeing, our separate personal plans. None of that. We just made it very clear that we were to respect our home by not bringing any relations in especially with romantic intentions! Taboo!!! So I thought!!!

While we had talked about divorce, we did not pursue it for many reasons: Not good time to sell, Or we could keep the house and we come and go as we please. He also had a lot of equipment for his Ham Radio volunteering activities and to sell would mean he had to find a place big enough to get them all in. No such luck and with our relationship being platonic I should not have cared and pushed on the divorce. There was also one thing I had in mind and that was my gratitude for all the years we were together and even the simplest act of love or kindness remained inside me and I am not one to forget that. There is such a thing as gratefulness for all the years he changed my life for the better. That is something I cannot deny and with his age and health issues, my conscience sometimes whispers! It is easy to blame someone than to put the blame on oneself and I was fully aware of my shortcomings and frailty as I was aware of his! There is always two sides to a coin!

There were many situations that pushed me against the wall and as soon as I became the goat of my Zodiac sign, I would begin to attack like a goat that had reached the top of the mountain and has no other way to go but forward! Here is one situation that will prove that! After seventeen years of being married, I asked Tony to add my name to the Title of the property. He refused. No matter what explanation I made, he still refused so I told him I was going to consult a Lawyer and he said "go ahead" and I did!

The woman lawyer I saw in Rancho Cucamonga asked me at the end of our session if I would just let her write him a letter or give him a chance to personally appear to discuss the issue. Because of my fair disposition I decided to give Tony a chance to present himself so an appointment was made.

The morning of our appointment, he asked me to postpone our appointment as he said he did not sleep well and his stomach was bothering him, so I rescheduled a couple of days later. Come day of our appointment, he said: "Best if we drove separate cars" and I said "Why? Are you going somewhere after the meeting?" He said, "No. It is best we did that" and I said okay, just follow me!

At the lawyer's office, he sat down with his shoulders looking very tense and he looked uneasy. Then the lawyer spoke: "I just want you both to know that I am not representing Marcia and I am not representing you Tony. I am here to mediate and come to a solution with Marcia's concern over the property". As soon as she said that, Tony gave a deep sigh and said "I thought I was here to sign papers". The lawyer explained how I decided to give him an opportunity to present himself. I think that made him see another side of me because throughout the meeting he became agreeable and cooperative. He agreed that my name should be added to the Title and other matters of importance were discussed and we left solving a simple problem that was right and legal.

While my heart felt at peace, our relationship stayed stagnant. We were both very involved in Volunteering but with different organizations. Tony was a very active volunteer for the Salvation Army, the Chino Hills Search and Rescue and with the Ham Radio club. When 9/11 happened he was asked to go to Ground Zero for two weeks and he took photos of the devastations of that fateful event of the Twin Towers in New York, He also went to Oklahoma when a big earthquake destroyed their cities. He had gone to Honduras to help with the Salvation Army take care of the very rural areas and bring medical help to those who were far from civilization.

I, on the other hand, was very involved with the American Cancer Society with their very successful Relay For Life where I chaired six events in the cities of Claremont, Chino Hills and my very own city of Chino. From there I became a Legislative Ambassador for their sister organization, American Cancer Society Cancer Action Network. There I was able to travel to Sacramento and Washington D.C. to speak to our Legislators and Senators on issues that are related to cancer. It was a Passionate endeavor and to this day I will still say, "I cannot think of representing another cancer Organization but ACS for this organization is a huge Pie and each piece represents the many faces of Cancer. I also believe that both ACS and ACSCAN are vehicles that goes in many directions but only Leads and ends to finding the cure to cancer".

Our marriage lasted but it held no relationship. We were there for each other but we did not spend much time together and I believe that was the road towards our total detachments as husband and wife. We were not unhappy but we were not joyful either. Slowly, we just became roommates. Our issues became monetary. Whenever Tony gave me cash for groceries, at least twice a day he would ask me when I would go food shopping. When I asked him why he is so concerned, he had said that because I did not use the money for what it was intended for. So I got mad. I was insulted.

I then told him that I was not going to do the food shopping anymore and for him to do it. His answer was a surprise to me. He said "why don't I just give you money and you buy what you want and I will just go buy what I want!" Was that suppose to be a reason to argue? Nope!!! So it began. He also had gone to family reunions where he did not want me to go. When he got there he would call me and let everyone talk with me! Was that a part of his meanness? With that I kept it all In. Resentment found its place in my bones and I became an expert in clamming up or a goat that had reached the top! The indifference of his attitude towards me made me stronger, prouder and basically quite independent. One thing he never deprived me of are any medical needs. But if I am sick, if I do not make myself something to eat, I would starve. He never offered to get me something to eat because he does not know how to cook. The only one time he ever did something for me to eat was to put the popcorn bag in the microwave! That was all!!!

"Learning not to expect is the key to not getting disappointed." Knowing how to get your way is another art one has to learn in a marriage or a relationship. I learned it after all these years and I also used it only when necessary. Like most men, Tony resents being told what to do. The key is to plant the seed and then wait a while to see it sprout as though it was their idea. Men do not want to be rushed or disturb when they are doing something especially when football is on. The key? Wait for the right time to ask and say "if you have time, can you ....??? More often than not, you will get your way.

More often than not, a marriage or a relationship that has soured, cannot be sweet again but there is that possibility of being amicable and more cautious in dealing with one another. So Tony and I became friends and we lived apart most of the time. I had places to stay and my freedom from any matrimonial obligations were boxed and keyed and never to be opened again. We were kinder to each other and somehow could communicate better and agreed mostly on things regarding the house.

I was there for Tony when he needed a stent to be placed. I saw a worried look on his face so I asked him "are you scared?" and he said he was, with the thought that they may saw open his chest. He looked so helpless in that emergency room bed with his blue gown and blue hair cover. When he had a bad bladder stone attack, he was bent over with pain, wrenching and throwing up before he got into the car. As soon as he was taken in, he was given a strong pain killer shot which calmed him down some. They scheduled him for surgery the next morning, so he told me to go home and he would call me in the morning to alert me about his surgery. Everything went well and at home I helped him with what needed to be done post-op.

He healed quickly and beautifully. Once he could walk around the house, he asked me to just buy him soup and jello and food that are easy to eat. He was very well stocked!

Tony never had good skin. He was not a vain person and he just was not into protecting his face when he is biking or mowing the half acre open field and half acre front and back lawn of our house. Even with the availability of the best skin care product I was selling (Jafra) Tony never took advantage of that to nourish his skin. So a couple of years ago, he was diagnosed with Melanoma and it was cancerous. It did not seem to bother him. He just goes for his regular check ups and he is fine. When I see him I look at his face and head for any signs of growth and sometimes I see something and would mention it to him and he would just say "I have an appointment with my dermatologist"! That is how we are and will be until the winds of change come again to disturb us.

My life has changed so much since that fateful day in April 2005 when Tony told me "We just Co-Exist!" There was no hurt feelings simply because I have detached myself emotionally from him as my husband. I did not expect it that is for sure and I have accepted the level of relationship that has now entered my life. Funny thing is this sudden change in our marriage set us both free to be happier and to be more caring towards each other without obligated expectations.

We talked of divorce yes, but we never pursued it. There was still this mutual feeling of being married yet living separate lives. One of the important aspect of this change was my basic concern for respect of our household. I told him that in our separate lives, we must agree that neither one of us will bring someone in the house who will sleep over. I emphasize to him that we must agree to exercise respect for our home of over twenty years. Whatever we did personally for our happiness or just plain living life after being on a "co-exist" arrangements is our business and we must respect that as well.

Since this declaration of mutual freedom and living apart for convenience of our health and well being, we have become much better friends. We were both there for each other. I come and go and he has a schedule of his own that does not include me. I treasure our home that I made beautiful and comfortable for our way of life. The small orchard that I created with fruits of my taste, was always there to greet me whenever I come and each plant and trees I talk to seem to welcome me home. We have become better people to each other and Tony has taken his responsibility towards my health needs. It is definitely cheaper than him paying me alimony and I believe he knows that now.

Without having our own children made it easier for this change. We had Matilda, the mutt and Daisy, the Chow and of course Keetee, the cat that adopted us. All of them are gone now but are within our home, out there in the out-field where they used to play and roam. We miss them for each one of them gave us unconditional joy. Now we have Peggy Sue, the Farrell cat who came out from the garage with Matilda. They had become very close and always sleeping together that when Matilda became sick and had to be put to sleep, Peggy Sue mourned. To this day, I am not quite sure if she has passed that mourning stage but one thing is for sure, Peggy Sue has no desire to be there in the patio where she and Matilda used to sleep together. That I think is a good indicator that she still miss her and has no intentions of being out there without her dear friend Matilda. One thing noticeable is her joy in watching the birds drink or take a bath in that small water holder I created so they may stop and replenish and cleanse their bodies as they continue their never-ending flight to nowhere!!!

As for me, my life will go on and I will enjoy every moment of it. This change in my marital status that Tony had chosen for us, has its blessings. My heart is not closed, for inside there is no bitterness but understanding for our mutual needs. Am I happy? Of course! Arrangements sometimes between two people serve a good purpose and it seemed that way for us. Marriage is not just about living together. It is living together with harmony and respect. Love and Care are like a horse and a carriage. You can't have one without the other and I believe we have that even in a smaller dosage but good enough to know when one needs the other for help and compassion.

My horizon is far and wide and my journey will continue where adventures await me and perhaps someone may be around the bend waiting just for me with my new life in his hands. Until then, God is with me and I know with HIM in my life, nothing else but goodness and blessings will encase my life so no more storm shall come, but to pass!

## Panta Rhei!
## <u>The Power of Acceptance!</u>

"Sometimes the best way to free yourself from a burden is to accept it." Much of the destructive situation comes from fighting against it. Once you stop fighting, you can start progressing. Certainly if there is a threat, you protect yourself against it. But there is no point fighting against what already is. When you accept the situation, that is the starting point at which you begin to make the most of it. When you can go beyond acceptance into sincere gratitude, you take on a powerful positive momentum. In short, accept what is, then find something positive about it. "Even the most desperate situation has its positive aspects and possibilities." You'll uncover them only after you've accepted that the situation exists. "Acceptance is not surrender. It is the recognition of reality." By clearly seeing what is, by acknowledging and even being grateful, you can move things forward toward the way you would like them to be!

Front view of the house where I grew up in: Top is the bedroom where I slept. Bottom is the den/library. Right hand corner is that very door that I slowly pushed open and where my mother stood, handing me the small suitcase that would change the course of my life and destination. Not a good memory!

View from the street. 663 J. Wright St. San Juan, Rizal Philippines. Masters bedroom. There is a veranda that was accessible yet hidden in the closet. Hardly anyone goes there but me as I would scoot down from a tiny opening only to pick ripe pomelo for my mom who personally peeled these white pomelo and slice by slice she would peel and chill to serve my dad. We had our own pomelo tree. Pink in color and sweet but not as sweet as the white one only meant for my dad and mom.

This is the terrace which is L-Shaped. Almost every weekend we had a party where dancing is the main reason. Us younger kids learned to dance by using a towel and wrapping it around the post and pretending it was our partner.

The Veranda! Big bay windows of the masters bedroom. Very secured.
Plants and trees are my mother's Labor of Love even with the presence of
our gardener!

My mother's three stages of life beginning at age 20. A beauty to behold.

My grandmother Maria Yusi with daughter Pilar and grand daughter Alma.

With her sisters in law: Imang Ariang (Maria $ Bundalian in red. Imang Vitang Datu in black. Imang Piang (Pilar) Del Rosario in stripes. Imang Toreng (Victoria) Castro in white. "Imang" is a form of respects that stands for "mother. My dad only had one brother, Apolinario Bundalian, the sweetest uncle I have ever known.

My mother with her parents: Maria Valdez and Jose Rivera. Sadly, I never knew much about my grandmother and I wished my mother was here still so she could share unique stories about her!

With me are the two most important Mothers in the World. My biological Mother Marciana in the middle and my adoptive Second Mother Nena.

## **<u>Venture Out!</u>**

"When faced with a choice, choose the path that strengthens you." Choose to learn, choose to grow, choose to more fully become who you are. Explore places you have never not been before. Look at ideas and concepts that you have nor considered before.

If you stay hidden in the comfortable and familiar, your spirit can soon grow weary. Venture out and recharge the passion in your life. Venture out there beyond routine and expected. Venture out and discover the depth and richness of who you are.

"A life that is tested and challenged is a life that surely becomes filled with real purpose." The more briskly the wind blows against your face, the more fully alive you'll feel.

Venture out from where you've been, then from that new perspective, venture out again. There is no end to what you can discover and become. ( Ralph Matson )

## Positive Alternatives! ( Easy to say but it can be done!)

Rather than being annoyed, be amused. Instead of getting angry, become curious. In place of envy, feel admiration. In place of worry, take action. In place of doubt, have faith.

"Negative energy is just positive energy that is flowing in the opposite direction." There is no need to fight or run away from this negative energy. All you need to do is change its direction.

The more negative you are, the more positive you can be, An automobile that can travel 70 miles per hour to the East can also travel just as fast when going West. But first, someone must turn it around.

When you sense yourself becoming negative, stop and consider what it would mean to apply that negative energy in the opposite direction.

Turn your sadness into caring. Transform your complaints into useful suggestions. Change your bitterness into determination. The energy is already there. All you need to do is change its direction!

## And This Prayer Before Sleep

**Dear God!**
**As I lay me down to sleep, Relax the tension of my body.**
**Calm the restlessness of my mind, still the**
**thoughts which worry and perplex me.**
**Help me to rest myself and all my problems**
**in your strong and loving arms.**
**Let your spirit speak to my mind and heart while I**
**sleep so that when I wake up in the morning,**
**I may find that I have received in the night time:**
**Light for my Way, Strength for my Trials, Peace**
**for my Worries, Forgiveness for my Sins,**

**Grant me sleep tonight,**
**And tomorrow ~ Power to Live in Jesus Name. Amen.**

## <u>WHAT DO YOU CHOOSE?</u>

To each of us is given the Power to be Strong.
The Power to be Weak or to be Right or Wrong.
We all have the Power to Win or to Lose,
What do you choose?

To each of us is promised
The Best Things in Life
Peace and Contentment
And Freedom from Strife.
Now all these things are ours to Accept or Refuse,
What do you Choose?

We can have our Blessings
Just as long as we give
If only we start right now
Then our Blessings will live.
No matter who you are
Or what your age
Or where you have been
It's never too late, never too late
To let the Sun Shine In!
To each of us is offered
The mighty Help of God.
For He's the One who made us
From just a Bit of Sod.

So have Faith and Be Happy
Fear and Prepare to Lose
What do you Choose?
Now all these things are ours to Accept Or Refuse!

*****

**Que Sera, Sera,** What Will Be Will be.
The Future is not ours to see,
**Que Sera, Sera!**

My Journey has a Path and Around the Bend is
Someone Who Will Change My Life Again!
Marcia Genoveva Bundalian
July 5, 2018

## <u>May 25, 2019</u>

How time flies when you are having fun!

But was I really only having fun since 10 months ago when I thought I would be done with my book?

Realistically it was not all fun but it was a rude awakening moment for me.

Moments that made me think of what else do I really want out of this stage of my life.

Freedom came to mind. Putting higher value to myself and to be selfish for once in my life!

It was after all had left after our Thanksgiving family get together where it was pure warmth and love for each other was in the air. I sat there in the living room alone, looking at the cleaned tables and kitchen that everyone had taken part in making sure I had nothing else to do after they left.

It felt good and I suddenly came to the realization that things will be done even if I do not lift a hand. My sister Ludette, my son Tyrone, my daughter Mia, my daughter-in-law Rachel, my son-in-law Ricky, and my grandsons Vincent and Enzo all were moving like production line, all having taken a chore, big and small.

It was very quiet and my mind was speaking loud to me. "Free yourself" it said. "You have done so much already. It is time to relinquish, time to step back, time to move forward with what Marcia want. So I listened and before Christmas came, my daughter Mia asked me via text what were our plans for Christmas and my first response was "I have no plans!" I just message them that all I want this time was to celebrate Christmas as it should be celebrated. No gifts, no fuss, no stress! Simple.

I told them I was making plans with my other friends to go away and abandon. Give our family the moment for them to evaluate our presence in their lives. Not to be taken for granted because we are always there for them. It was time for us to put ourselves before them and let them take the lead. I told my family I was taking a break! My son's reaction was "Have a good time Ma!" and my daughter's reaction was "But Christmas would not be the same without you!"

Sadly our plans fell off the horse's back as two of my friends succumbed to the guilt trip their family put them through! My daughter in law Rachel called me and said "We will go there and bring food and you do not have to do anything, We just want to be with you". So they came and every time I was in the kitchen a voice would say "you are not suppose to be here Ma." So my wonderful family came through with flying colors. It was then I knew that my decision was founded and my life will be as I want it to be for that moment and time. I could move on!

My heart was calm, my mind begun to de-clutter. What else should I do to make this progressive mind on the right track? And it dawn on me that for the last two visits I made at my house in Chino, I was raving mad at Tony. The reasons why may sound petty but to me they were disrespectful of me and my representation in that house. When I am there I become a cleaning lady and when I leave, the kitchen, living room, my office, my bedroom and bathroom are all cleaned. My office, bedroom and bathroom doors are shut as no one has any business going in there! So when I saw my office door open and the room was a mess, I stormed out and asked Tony why my office door was open and his answer to me was "Peggy Sue, his cat is bored so she needed another place to explore!" Oh My God!

I lost it! My mouth was like a machine gun that saw no end! It made me more mad when he said "Well, you are not here anyway"." Excuse Me!" I said. "Have you forgotten that you were the one who told me we just co-exist and that we go our separate ways and do our own thing? Were you not the one who told me I could come and go as I please? You have disrespected my space because you obviously value the cat more than me so let us just finish this and let us divorce! I am done!"

The second time was more recent. When I arrived and as I opened the gate, I noticed that my beautiful Madagascar plant that I started as a tiny little starter but now is expensive because of its size. He said he had to cut it because it was leaning forward. I asked what he did with the branches and he said I put them on the trash! That was it! All hell broke loose and my machine gun mouth was shooting words he had heard before and one of them was "I am done Tony. Let us divorce and sell this property. He said "I do not want to sell it" so I said you are not the only party here! He said "You have a place go, I don't" and I said "That is not my problem!" So it was cast! We will divorce amicably and without prolonging the agony and making our lawyers richer than us! It was his decision to buy me out! I could not be any happier!

My clogged mind was clear, my heart was light. My spirit was sad. As I started going through my personal stuff that I planned to take when the divorce is decreed, my stereo played songs that hit home and soon I realized tears were coming down my face. My life with Tony was not riddled with emotional ups and downs but rather it was lived with total independence and with him never telling me "No, you cannot do that!" We once talked about this matter and he said to me "Marcia, nobody should stop any one for doing what they want to do". And so our marriage survived with total understanding and more so respect for our individualities. But with that came a slow detachment of physical relationship and while we remained as a couple the reality of it all is it was not in the true sense of the word.

I met with a divorce lawyer with Tony's awareness and open mindedness. So when I got home I told him about my consultation and we both came to the conclusion that it will not be a contested divorce. The morning after, I again felt some ache in my heart as I looked out my window and seeing the backyard that my hands and sweat created my personal garden and I heard a voice saying to me "it is time to let it go!" I felt sad still. I went to the den where Tony was and I said to him I needed to talk with him for a few minutes. He turned off his computer and turned around to face me.

I said to him "No matter where this process of divorce is going to take us, I want you to know that should you ever need me for emergency reasons, you can count on me. I want us to part without animosity but friends for I have no reason to hate you or be angry with you and I believe you have no reasons as well". To that he agreed with me. Then I continued "I have been in transient for 15 years now and I cannot handle it anymore. I need to be free, to be happy and to create my own life without any baggage to carry like before. While our marriage did not work and last, we still had good times to remember and smile but we need to move forward, do you agree?" To that he said "I agree."

Now I was crying and Tony got up and extended his arms and said "come here and let me give You a hug." For the first time in almost 20 years, we embraced and he was consoling. As we stepped away from each other, I saw his eyes and nose were red. I knew then that Tony really cared for me and that we have become friends for a reason, and a season. You see, Tony has cancerous Melanoma and he has stents to unclog his clogged arteries. But he remains active yet realistic.

As I left my Chino house the next day and drove with my music on Escape, I felt free. Everything about me was clear. The sky was blue and while the temperature outside was summer hot inside my car was the coolness of emotions, and it felt like God had opened the windows of my life and set everything free! A new horizon was before me and I know there was no turning back. Finally, Tony and I set ourselves free from a life together that really was going nowhere. It is now just a matter of time and soon my new journey will begin! Que Sera, Sera. What Will Be Will Be!

"Love is a Positive Feeling and if one cultivates this
feeling in their life, they will surely free themselves from
any unbalanced condition that surrounds them."
(Syd Banks )

The curtain of my first book shall come to a close and with that I would like to share with you my readers, a poem that has settled in my mind, my hearts and my outlook. I chose to put this at the end for in here is where I will find that one consoling feeling that no matter where the wind blows, no matter where my path takes me, My Lord God of All Creations shall be by my side, stirring me in HIS gentle and loving ways to that centered road where nothing but blessings awaits me. Come walk with me and together let us Find My Other Shoe!

## *FOOTPRINTS*

*One night I dreamed I was walking*
*along the beach with the Lord.*
*Many scenes from my life flashed across the sky.*
*In each scene I noticed footprints in the sand.*
*Other times there were one set of footprints.*

*This bothered me because I noticed that during the low*
*periods of my when I was suffering from anguish, sorrow,*
*or defeat, I could only see one set of footprints/*

*So I said to the Lord, "YOU promised me Lord, that if*
*I followed You, You would walk with me always. But I*
*have noticed that during the most trying period of my life*
*there have only been one set of footprints in the sand.*

*"Why, when I needed You most, have You not been there for me?"*
*The Lord replied.*

*"The years when you have seen only one set of*
*footprints in the sand, Is when I carried you."*

*With humility and deep gratitude I bow*
*my head to You, My Lord.*
*Your Daughter Forever.*

*Marcia*

There I am seated in the middle because I was the tallest among the girls.

This time I am standing in the middle.

There I am seated almost in the middle because I was the tallest among the girls.

This time I am standing in the middle. It is amazing how we (Wellington, third left on the floor) (Virgie in ponytail) Aurora third girl, second row) Me, the tallest one  Tessie, third row, second to the left have managed to remain in touched after we had a school reunion in Vegas in 2005.

This photo was taken at our garden in the Philippines before we left for our school, St. John's Academy, a private non-sectarian school, owned and run by the Marquez family, where we all studied until we graduated in high school. In the photo is my older sister Vilma Damasca and younger sister, Fatima Victoria.

We wore our costumes to dance with at our Loyalty Day!

Here we are. Four sisters: Vilma Damasca in black. Marcia Genoveva in white blouse. Fatima Victoria in Polka dots. Lourdes Celerina with arms akimbo! Missing in this photo is our oldest sister Leila. The best and sweetest sister in the world. Sadly, her life was returned to God too early in July 1957 in a fatal vehicular accident. She left three sons behind: Mario, Jose and Rene, all surnamed Mondonedo.

My brother Joey and my mother! He was the Apple of her eyes!

My book will not be complete without my cousin Paz Rivera Lascano's photo and all that I have to say about her. She is the daughter of my mother's brother Tatang Picion as I called him. My relationship with Paz begun one summer when my mother took me, my younger sisters Fatima and Ludette to her hometown, in the Northern region of the Philippines called Floridablanca, Pampanga. My mother's three siblings lived in the compound that was basically the home of their parents for so many years. Imang Suling Luna lived in the big house with her family and my grandfather Jose Rivera, while Tatang Picion Rivera and Imang Sating Almario had their own houses. Here in this very compound all my childhood memories begun. Here was where I found the best cousin in the world. A few years younger than me, Paz was very shy especially because we were considered on a higher bracket of living and because my mother married a Civil Engineer and she was the only one among her siblings and cousins who moved from the province to the city when they got married. Comparatively speaking, my mother was considered a socialite because of my father's respectable position in the Senate. So when we go for a visit, all her cousins doted on her and us. My mother was a somebody!

Paz and I spent a lot of times up on a tree, especially one called "santol" a sour fruit that made us pucker our lips. We would climb the tree and find a safe place to sit with our legs dangling and rocking to ad fro. The best part of that climb was picking the fruit and with salt wrapped in paper, we would eat to our heart's content until our lips would turn pale from the salt. Sometimes, together with other cousins or friends we would run to the dried rice field until we get to a little river where we would catch little fish with our bare hands. Sometimes a train with sugar cane would come along and the boys would chase it until they have pulled some sugar cane that we all shared. One time I did not realize I was standing on an ant hill until the ants started biting my legs. I went back crying because it was so painful and Paz was so sweet in trying to console me. That was the last time I went to that dried rice field again!

Every summer for three months, Paz and I shared the best time ever. We never fought. She was always looking after me as I did her. Then we grew up. But we never drew apart and one day I learned that she was going to stay with us during the duration of her college years. Like my mother, Paz was the only one among her siblings who flew out of the nest and talked to her father to allow her to go to the city to study. Objection due to safety and distance was met with more determination. So she won. While living with us, she earned her keep and my parents treated her like she was their own especially my father who just loved having relatives live with us because they want to further their education. Our house was their home and all were grateful for the goodness of heart of my parents.

Paz became a grade school teacher and one day she approached me about a school project. She needed to produce a play for her class. So I went to work. I did not realize then that someday I would be a writer. The Play I created won Second Place! I took Paz with me at my acting performances with the University of the Philippines Mobile Theater and she loved it because they thought she was my chaperone! I always felt safe with her around me. If there was something I needed, I did not have to ask her. That's how sensitive she was to my needs and we both loved to eat, a pleasure we both enjoyed. We both became mothers almost at the same month, me with my daughter Mia and her with her first born Rowena.

To this day we have remained very close. We have not forgotten to laugh so hard we could not even understand what the other is saying. She knows me more than my sisters do. Paz was my best friend then and even now. Nothing has changed between us and the love we share is pretty special because it is so unconditional and so kind and so sincere. She is one hell of a mother to Rowena, Raymond and Ryan and so devoted a wife to her loving husband Ben. She is happy and as she deserves to be and I am happy because I have a cousin who thinks the world of me as much as I think of her that way!

One of the joys of visiting Paz is picking her home grown "macopa"! Just delicious and mouth watering!

My best of the Best cousin Paz Rivera Lascano and I during our younger years!

Taken at Daly City to celebrate our cousin Cely Luna Araneta's 75th birthday! Our mutual affection to each other had weathered time and distance. Our Bond continues to be tight!

My Debut. My older sister Vilma who had a dress shop created my dress with Flowers made of straw.

My brother Joey and I.

My childhood friends: Tina de la Concepcion Aura Marcelo Vicky Johnson Jojo de la Concepcion Perry Martinez, next to Jojo

Here I am on the right with the former First Lady Imelda Romualdez-Marcos. Taken at the SSS Auditorium, QC at the Foundation Day event where we, UP Mobile Theater performed with the late Professor Wilfredo Maria Guerrero directing and producing his well known Plays. First Lady was on a campaign trail for her husband former President Ferdinand Marcos then a Senator running for the presidency. Next to me is fellow thespian Manny Abad.

My two sisters Ludette, our youngest and Fatima, second to the youngest who in 1978 has walked in God's heavenly kingdom and my adorable niece Pinky Joson my flower girl, now a Mejia.

My ever loving parents whose dignified characters molded me into who I am today and my first niece Pinky who also was guided by their love.

My Precious Jewels. My Treasures. My Life. Mina Patricia and Tyrone Paquito (named after my dearest mother in law Paquita Concepcion Matta)

Daddy with his favorite little people! Patricia Gemma Torres Mom: Ludette Manny Boy Soriano Mom: Fatima. Rowena Lascano (red) Mom: Paz Rivera Tyrone and Mia Matta Mom: Marcia

Me carrying my nephew Manny Boy Soriano. A gift to us from my departed sister Fatima Victoria.

Tisa and Me

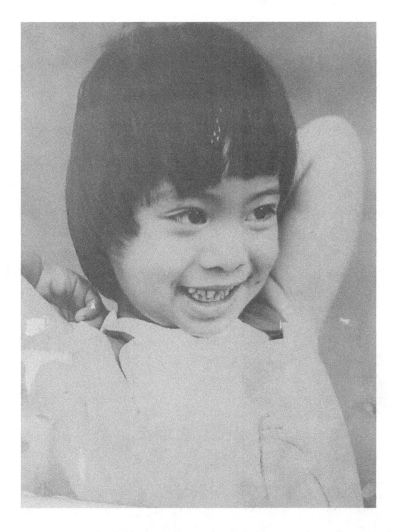

Patricia Gemma Bundalian Torres My third child through my love for this cute and adorable child of my sister Ludette. Tisa, as she was fondly called was the baby in the household and she ruled! Spoiled rotten but loved with a tinge of discipline. As an adult, Tisa excelled in all her choices in life. I saw her as a cheerleader for this girl could dance. Her sweetness and high pitch tone were perfect combination and her smile and eyes were the heart and soul of her being. At 36. God reached out to her and she took HIS hand. Peace and everlasting life was the gift God gave her for trusting HIM and following HIS lead. She left two beautiful children. Alyssa and Zion Cherry.

Pinning the chicken tail costume of my son Tyrone before they danced at our school St. John's Academy.

My second Mother Nena Gomez. She was my best friend too and I miss her terribly. With her are her little chickies; Tyrone, Mia and Tisa.

My oldest sister Leila passed away at a very young age of 24 in a very bad vehicular accident leaving behind three sons: Rene, who was a baby then and was running a high fever that made my sister leave work hurriedly; I have not seen Rene close to 50 years who now resides in Europe, Billy who resides in the Philippines where his successful businesses undertakings ties him down and Jose, who studied dentistry and now is a flight attendant internationally!

At the Manila International Airport December 27, 1976 as I waved to my toddlers Tyrone and Mia on my way to New York to marry my beloved Leroy Perry Kramer, my knight is shining armor! The man who lovingly changed the course of my life and the lives of my children. Lee changed our world and made it a better place to be.

Walking down the aisle at daughter Nancy Kramer's wedding.

Dancing with my late husband Lee Perry Kramer. He gifted me with a bracelet with a sweet message "You are the Best thing that Ever Happened to Me!" We made beautiful memories together and Lee will always be My Knight in Shining Armor!

Lee and I loved to dance and he can dance! Best
dancing partner ever! March 27, 1980.

Chicago

New York

Tennessee

Ireland, 1978 Bunratty Castle where we ate Medieval Age style! With bare hands.

That's me gearing for dear life as I reached up to kiss the Blarney Stone in Ireland.

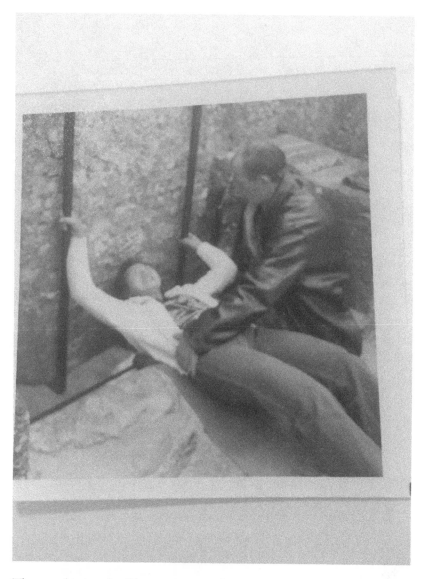

They say kissing the Blarney Stone will give you the Gift of Gab and I tell you they are so right for when I went back to New York I was a changed person!

Blarney Castle, five miles north of Cork, became famous when Queen Elizabeth I said, "It's the usual blarney," of Lord Blarney's persuasive but hollow chatter. Visitors to the castle who aspire to the gift of the gab stretch backward at a dizzying height to kiss the Blarney Stone.

Left, tourist kissing the Blarney Stone;

This is the clipping of the Blarney Stone in Ireland.

Tony and I both lost our spouses to cancer almost at the same time. He in California and me in New York. Six years after my second husband Lee passed away, my daughter Mia and I moved to Southern California where my sister Lourdes and her husband Larry Crisler lived and took my son Tyrone to live with them after a very bad fight he had with his father who had come back to his life too late. My gratitude to my sister and Larry so deep that a mere thank you is not enough!

New Year's Eve here we come! Not sure what year it was. My first husband was a Protestant who had to convert to Catholicism in order for us to be married in church My second husband Lee was Jewish and we got married at a Judge's chamber. If he did not pass away, we would still be living in New York. He changed my life forever. With my first marriage the ending was bitter and filled with anger with the immature man who traded his children for his freedom. To him I have said " he was a thorn that has been pricking me and it's removal was a blessing and a relief from a constant throbbing pain but thank God not to his children whose innocence of his departure was nothing but a mere gesture that left no meaning in their young lives and even now. With a Protestant and Jewish husbands, I had a conversation with God and asked him " Lord maybe I should marry someone who is a catholic like me. Maybe this time it will last?" So I accepted his proposal of marriage. So far we have been together for over a longer time. But this too shall end not because of nasty reasons but simply because we grew far apart yet we cared for each other to be there for each other.

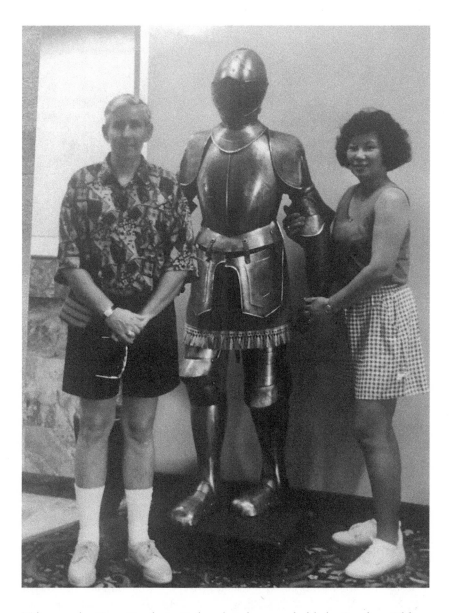

Taken at the Gray Castle in Colorado where we held the Stephen Sibling Reunion. This is where we all stayed. I miss my sweet sister in law Julie whose closeness to me I cherished and enjoyed. I miss our long hours of chatting over the phone and the laughters we shared.

There were four of us, who shared unconditional friendship: Elena Habaluyas who just turned 85 last August and who remained a true friend since we met in 1980 where she was hired to care for my then very sick husband Lee Perry Kramer who later died from cancer in August 1980 Nilda Magat whose whereabouts has become a total mystery. Evelyn Sinjian who was at that Korean Airlines 007 flight that was shot down during its flight. Both Elena and Nilda flew from New York and came to my wedding in 1989!

Taken at the Jafra Cosmetics International event where I was announced Top in the Nation in Sponsoring! If a picture could count a thousand words, this is it!!!

My Jafra Cosmetics Family: Adelina Adams, Kathy Maroste, my director in red, Me. Behind: Amber Kraus, Tom Maroste, Janice Ross (next to Tom) Elvira West in white.

LAS VEGAS ........... 2000

FLASHING THE NUMBER THREE FINGER SIGNS AFTER I SAW
MY PICTURES ON THE BIG SCREEN !

THREE WEEKS BEFORE THE END OF THE CONTEST, I WAS IN
THE TOP 10. THE NUMBER ONE PLACE WAS TOO FAR FOR ME
TO CATCH UP SO I WAS WILLING TO SETTLE FOR SECOND OR
THIRD. I FOUND OUT I WAS IN NUMBER 6!

WHEN WE ARRIVED AND I REGISTERED, MY PACKET HAD A
RIBBON WITH NUMBER 5 IN IT. I KNEW THEN THAT I WAS IN
THE TOP FIVE.

AS THEY ANNOUNCED THE TOP FIVE I WAITED FOR MY NAME
FOR NUMBER FIVE, THEN FOUR.....THEN I HEARD IT LIKE THUNDER
"AND NUMBER THREE IN THE NATION FOR PERSONAL SPONSORING
IS MARCIA STEPHEN" AND ALL THREE BIG SCREEN HANGING FROM TH'
CEILING FLASHED MY PICTURE. WHAT A MOMENT TO REMEMBER AND
TO THINK I WAS SO SICK THAT DAY THAT AFTER THE SESSION
I WENT BACK TO THE HOTEL AND STAYED THERE THE ENTIRE
WEEK-END.

WHEN MY FRIEND KAROL STROMMEN CAME BY AND BROUGHT
ME DINNER, I MANAGED TO GIVE HER A FACIAL AND SIGN HER
UP. SINCE THEN I HAVE BEEN TEASED ABOUT SPONSORING
ANYONE EVEN WHEN I AM SICK IN BED!

This was taken in Las Vegas at our Jafra Cosmetics Conference  where i
was announced as Number Three in the Nation for Sponsoring. It was my
passion to make every woman I meet feel good about themselves by simply
showing them how they can enhance their God given beauty with simple
skin care routine and also showed them there is money that goes with their
improvement no matter what level they choose to do it.

My three fingers showed my excitement as my face was flashed on three big
TV screen. What a moment to remember!

MY FAMILY JEWELS: SON TYRONE AND DAUGHTER MIA

My beautiful and precious treasures and gifts from God!

We are One!

My son Tyrone, My daughter Mia and Me!

My son Tyrone and Me.

Tyrone was born eight pounds one ounce after a very long labor that started in the morning and ended with a c-section at eight in the evening.

When the nurse brought him to me, he looked like an eskimo baby. He is now towering with the height of almost 6 feet.

My daughter Mia and Me

Mia was a premature baby, born at eight months and she weighed only 4 lbs one ounce and was in the incubator for 23 days and in the nursery for a week until I was able to hold her when my mother and I took her home. The saying "small but terrible" does not apply to her but rather this says it all: " Mia is small but incredible!"

My handsome son Tyrone and his very pretty bride and wife Rachel Legaspi
Matta.

My beautiful daughter and her soul mate husband Ricky Yoingco.

My son Tyrone, whose character and personality traits he inherited from my father, with his two awesome nephews, My first grandson Vincent Ryan Pijuan ( Father: Tony Pijuan, cousin of former Miss Philippines, AuAu Pijuan ) and My pianist second grandson, Ricardo Lorenzo Yoingco who I fondly call Enzo! ( Father: Ricardo Yoingco Sr.)

My youngest sister Ludette Crisler and I.

Sightseeing at Joshua Tree! Brought in boxed lunch and we had a ball. We all became young again though not daring to hike or climb the beautiful mountains. Kneeling is Wellington Ty. Behind are: Florencia Roque-Mangaoang, Aurora, Me, Virgie and Tess. Brother and sisters are we!

Schoolmates and Classmates are we. Front Row: Vicky Lopez, Aurora Pesigan-Rabuy, Marcia Bundalian-Stephen Back Row: Betsy Gil-Del Rosario, Ricardo Diaz, Teresita Canlas-Mendoza, Lut Marcelo-Helin and Maripaz Crespo-Eclarin. Held in Las Vegas August 2005.

Grateful for the Friendship!
Glad for the Unconditional Love we share!
Remembering the past with a smile and a sigh!

My classmates at the reunion I hosted in Palm Desert. Sitting next to me is Virginia Parales-Solis, Wellington Ty, Teresita Canlas-Mendoza, Aurora Pesigan-Rabuy.

# Chino Hills Relay for Life scheduled June 23-24

**By Melodie Henderson**

The American Cancer Society's Relay for Life isn't just about finding a cure, said Chino Hills event chairwoman Marcia Bundalian-Stephen. It's about the survivors, and their message of hope.

Chino Hills' second annual Relay for Life will take place on June 23-24 at Chino Hills High School. Last year's inaugural relay drew about 500 participants; this year Ms. Bundalian-Stephen expects to double that number.

Participants are invited to set up home base at "Tent City." Team members will take turns walking around the track for 24 hours.

"You don't have to have cancer to be involved in this relay," said Ms. Bundalian-Stephen. "The reason I have been very passionate about this relay is because of the survivors. That's what this relay is about."

The event kicks off with the survivors lap, in which those who are battling cancer or have beaten the disease make the first lap with their caregivers and families.

Those who died from the disease are honored in the evening during the luminaria ceremony. Sold by volunteers, each luminaria is decorated

*Marcia Bundalian-Stephen*

with the names of those who lost their battle. Placed around the track, they light the way for walkers and runners.

"Every year the number of survivors increases. That is very exciting, and very important to me," Ms. Bundalian-Stephen said.

While she has not personally battled cancer, she considers herself a survivor, because of the losses she has sustained.

"I lost my husband, my sister and my brother-in-law," she said.

While the event is three months away, preparations are under way, and teams are coming together.

Team members can register

or find a team at www.cancer.org by clicking on Chino Hills. A registration fee of $10 per person is charged. Cynthia Zezulka is in charge of team recruitment and can be reached at 262-9829. Survivor chairwoman Norma Quintanilla can be reached at (591) 206-7141. To purchase a luminaria for $10, contact Karen Smith at (951) 328-2380.

In kind donations are also accepted, and donations are also needed for the event. Desired items are food, drinks, canopies, chairs, tables and ice.

Live entertainment will be provided throughout the event, and entertainers are also needed.

"We are looking for bands, singers, educational and inspirational speakers, instrumentalists, comedians – just a variety of entertainers," Ms. Bundalian-Stephen said.

Those who wish to audition may contact Dee Ketner at 573-9035.

Chino's Relay for Life is planned Aug. 4-5 at Ayala Park. The city will host a relay kickoff event at 5:30 p.m. April 26 at the Chino Senior Center. It is a motivational event where team members can sign up and get information about Relay.

For information, call Brenda Siqueiros at (951) 300-1204.

This was a write up with the Champion Newspaper on Saturday, April 7, 2007!

One of the six Relay For Life event I chaired in Chino Hills. Other cities were Chino and Claremont! A fund raising event for the American Cancer Society to eliminate cancer as the number one killer of our society. The Mayors of the cities have given their full support for this weekend event, a 24 hour sleepless night of walking alone or as a team for we believe that cancer does not sleep and can enter a home no matter where and how.

We walk because we are on guard and are ready to fight the beast with all our passion and dedication and hope and support of everyone who wants this world to be cancer free!

Let us hold hands and walk together and be that strong force that will drive this disease away from us all!!!

Me and my very dear friend Elena Mamuyac Habaluyas taken at the home of her daughter Anna Vero in New York. Time has tested our friendship and it is timeless!!

My so special friends: Aiko Bachkus and Lorraine McCall as we lunched at the Classic Club's Bellatrix restaurant. Life without friends is like a garden without plants and flowers because friends beautify our lives and they enhance our spirits with their fragrance of unconditional friendship.

My circle of friends is endless and it is filled with joy and admiration for those whose character I never have to doubt.

Pickleball/Paddle Tennis Club Social
Photos by Taffy Golden & Valerie Weinstein

News & Views · https://www.scpdca.com/Community_Magazine

Next to dancing I love sports and pickleball has basically given
me the opportunity to play which is so similar to tennis.

*Pickleball Club Ladder League. Photo provided by Taffy Golden.*

My pickleball friends and challenges!

My Pickleball Family! Sun City Palm Desert

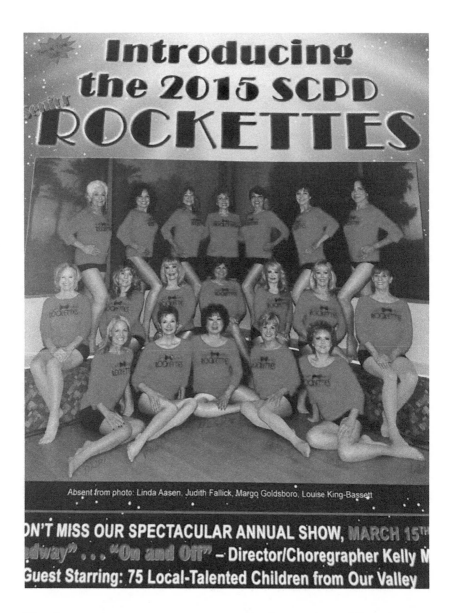

Here I am at the very center, sitting on the floor with my fellow dancers. Danced with the Sun City Palm Desert Senior Rockettes for three years. Memories were made of this!

Sun City Senior Rockettes Reunion luncheon at the Classic Club Bellatrix restaurant. In this photo are:

Left to Right:

Marcia, Donna, Denise, Kelly our director, Patty, Jinja, Sheryl, Claudette, Nancy, Cheryl and Marilyn.

It was great seeing everyone and looking back with pride and laughter, our days when dancing on stage was just a dream that became a reality with dedication, patience and gratitude.

We were a dancing family where we gave it our best and received the applause with such joy and endless love to music and dance! We are born to dance if only we would give it a try!

Marcia Genoveva Bundalian

# THE POWER OF A PRAYING WOMAN

Gods411

GOOD MORNING FATHER,

AS A MOTHER, WIFE AND WOMAN OF GOD
I LIFT MY FAMILY FIRST FOR PRAYER.
I KNOW THAT A WOMAN OF GOD
CAN MAKE A HUGE DIFFERENCE IN HER
FAMILY'S LIVES. BLESS OUR HOME LORD,
LET IT BE A HOME FULL OF YOUR BLESSINGS AND
PROVISIONS. LET IT BE A PLACE OF SAFETY AND LOVE.
WATCH OVER US AS WE SLEEP AND
PROTECT US FROM OUTSIDE EVIL.
MAY OUR HOUSE BE CLEANSED
AND FILLED WITH YOUR LOVE AND PEACE.
LET NO CHALLENGE TEAR US APART.
AS EACH ONE OF US STEPS OUT OF THE
DOOR I PRAY THAT EACH OF US
HAS THE ENERGY AND STRENGTH TO FACE TODAY'S
CHALLENGES. FILL EACH OF US WITH YOUR JOY
SO WE CAN BE A LIGHT IN THIS DARK
WORLD. REMIND EACH OF US THAT
WE WILL SUCCEED IN OUR DAY

AS LONG AS WE PUT YOU FIRST.
LORD, MAY MY CHILDREN HAVE AN
IMPACT ON LIVES AROUND THEM.
MAY YOUR WORD AND THEIR UPBRINGING
RING TRUE IN THEIR HEARTS.
PROTECT THEM FROM SATAN'S EVIL SCHEMES.
MAY YOUR SPIRIT ALWAYS CONVICT THEIR
HEARTS OF ANY LIES SATAN IS TELLING THEM.
CHILDREN CAN FALL AWAY FROM YOU,
I PRAY MINE STAY CLOSE TO YOUR COAT
TAILS SO THEY WILL ALWAYS KNOW YOU,
THE GOD OF LOVE.
LET ME BE A WOMAN OF STRENGTH, GRACE
AND MERCY FOR MY FAMILY LORD.
GIVE ME THE PATIENCE TO DEAL WITH
MY DAILY ROUTINE. LET MY HEART
REMEMBER YOUR WORD OF LOVE
WHEN I AM FEELING OVERWHELMED, TIRED,
UNAPPRECIATED AND UNLOVED.
YOU ARE THE GREAT PROVIDER AND PROTECTOR.
LET ME STAND AND FACE TODAY WITH COURAGE.
I AM A POWERFUL WOMAN OF GOD
AND A PRAYER WARRIOR FOR MY
FAMILY. HEAR MY PRAYER LORD
AND BLESS MY FAMILY. AMEN.